Life and Death

The Jones and Bartlett Series in Philosophy

Robert Ginsberg, EDITOR

Ayer, Sir Alfred J. • *The Origins of Pragmatism*—Studies in the Philosophy of Charles Sanders Peirce and William James

Ayer, Sir Alfred J. • *Metaphysics and Common Sense*

Baum, Robert J. • Rensselear Polytechnic Institute • *Philosophy and Mathematics*

De Lucca, John • Queen's University • *Reason and Experience—* Dialogues in Modern Philosophy

Ginsberg, Robert • The Pennsylvania State University, Delaware County • *Welcome to Philosophy*—A Handbook for Students

Hanson, Norwood Russell • *Perception and Discovery*—An Introduction to Scientific Inquiry

Hudson, W. D. • Exeter University • *Reason and Right*

Jason, Gary • San Diego State University • *Clear Thinking*—An Invitation to Logic

Pauling, Linus and Ikeda, Daisaku • *A Dialogue Between Linus Pauling and Daisaku Ikeda* • Translated and Edited by Richard L. Gage

Pojman, Louis P. • The University of Mississippi • *Life and Death: Grappling with the Moral Dilemmas of Our Time*

Pojman, Louis P. • The University of Mississippi • *Life and Death: A Reader in Moral Problems*

Ross, Stephen David • State University of New York, Binghamton • *Moral Decision*—An Introduction to Ethics

Veatch, Robert M. • The Kennedy Institute of Ethics, Georgetown University • *Cross-Cultural Perspectives in Medical Ethics*

Veatch, Robert M. • The Kennedy Institute of Ethics, Georgetown University • *Medical Ethics*

Life and Death

*Grappling with the Moral
Dilemmas of Our Time*

Louis P. Pojman
University of Mississippi

Jones and Bartlett Publishers
Boston   London

Editorial, Sales, and Customer Service Offices
Jones and Bartlett Publishers
20 Park Plaza
Boston, MA 02116

Jones and Bartlett Publishers International
PO Box 1498
London W6 7RS
England, UK

Library of Congress Cataloging-in-Publication Data

Pojman, Louis P.
    Life and death : grappling with the moral dilemmas of our time /
Louis P. Pojman.
       p. cm.
    Includes bibliographical references and index.
    ISBN 0-86720-334-X
    1. Death—Moral and ethical aspects. I. Title.
R726.P64 1992
174'.24—dc20
                                        92-3023
                                          CIP

Printed in the United States of America
95 94 93 92   10 9 8 7 6 5 4 3 2 1

To

Bob and Barbara Ascher
Sean Connor
Jean Freas
Dorothy Kellett
Eileen Letchworth
Bob Miness
Linda Ward
David and Ros Will
Judith Zinke
Jeannette and Alex Sanger
who in the spirit of Margaret Sanger
stood for moral integrity.
To these heroes of my heart,
this book is dedicated.

"And the Light shineth in darkness and darkness comprehended it not"
(John 1:5)

CONTENTS

PREFACE

This is a book about contemporary moral dilemmas that seeks to throw light on the subject from a philosophic point of view. Sophisticated technology creates new possibilities that our ordinary moral beliefs are not prepared to handle. On the one hand, medical expertise can prolong almost indefinitely physical life—but not mental life—on expensive ventilators. On the other hand, military expertise can destroy life at a record-setting rate. With the weakening of religious authority and the emergence of cultural pluralism, a multitude of possibilities present themselves on issues that go to the very heart of our personal and social existence. At present society is deeply divided on the matters of life and death discussed in this book: on the sanctity of life, the meaning of death and dying, suicide, euthanasia, abortion, the death penalty, animal rights, and war. This book uses philosophic analyses to replace heat with light on these burning issues.

Nothing is more important for our age, nothing is more inspiring for the thoughtful person, nothing is more challenging for our society than to think clearly, comprehensively, and imaginatively about the moral life. Little guidance is given ordinary people to enable them to evaluate and construct good moral reasoning. It is with this hope of shedding light on the moral life and equipping ordinary men and women to reflect critically on the moral dilemmas of our time that I have written this book.

The idea of writing a book on ethics for students first occurred to me in May 1987 when I read the *Time* magazine cover story "What Ever Happened to Ethics?" It was a story of the growing corruption, scandals, and hypocrisy permeating almost every aspect of American life. As I read newspaper and magazine articles on moral issues relating to death and dying, abortion, capital punishment, animal rights, and other related subjects, I was disturbed by bad arguments or dogmatic intuitions displayed on all sides of these matters.

For the past 15 years, while teaching ethics at the University of Notre Dame, the University of Texas at Dallas, and the University of Mississippi, and lecturing to the general public in schools and churches, I've discussed with students and lay people issues relating to life and death. I've learned much from them about these matters, and to my students in particular I have dedicated this book.

An anthology, *Life and Death: A Reader*, with selections on each topic

ix

discussed herein, accompanies this book and could well be used as a companion volume. However, either book could provide sufficient material for an entire course.

Joseph Betz, Forrester Church, Joseph DeMarco, John Jagger, Stephen Kaufman, Jim Landesman, Len Mitchell, Laura Purdy, Henry Sackin, Jeri Sechzer, and Mary Anne Warren made suggestions on improving an earlier draft of this work. Bob Ginsberg read through the entire manuscript twice, each time making penetrating criticisms and insightful suggestions. I cannot thank him enough. Art Bartlett is responsible for getting me to write this material up as a textbook. Angela Gladfelter was a joy to work with in producing the final manuscript. Most of all, I am grateful to my wife, Trudy, a Hospice nurse, who helped me with the material concerning death and the dying process and who has given me an example of how to live.

Much of the material here was given in a series of lectures at the Unitarian Church of All Souls in New York City, whose members provided a marvelous context for rethinking this material, some of whom took courageous moral stands which deeply inspired me throughout the writing of this work. To these friends this book is dedicated.

Louis P. Pojman

Department of Philosophy
University of Mississippi
University, MS 38677
August 14, 1991

Welcome to Moral Philosopy:
A Word to the Student

We are discussing no small matter, but how we ought to live.

—SOCRATES

Philosophy is the passionate pursuit of truth—literally, the love of wisdom. It begins with wonder at the mysteries and paradoxes of existence and seeks to arrive at informed judgments that enhance our understanding and lend meaning to life. It is revolutionary in that it often disrupts the received opinion of an age, calling on us to think new thoughts, critically, comprehensively, and honestly, even when they disturb deeply held biases. Its weapons are the swords of reason and imagination. Like science and mathematics it is a highly rational activity, centered on argument and analysis and disciplined thinking, but like art and drama it appeals to imagination and life experience in creating probing thought experiments, counterexamples to conclusions, and interdisciplinary applications of principles.

This book is a philosophic exploration into the moral status of crucial issues connected with our being alive and having to face the reality of death (either our own or that of others). Its topics include the idea of the sanctity of life versus the quality of life, the meaning of death, abortion, suicide, euthanasia, the death penalty, animal rights (do animals have a right to life?), and war. The last chapter deals with the very definition of "death." The issues are interrelated, all having as an underlying theme the question of what makes life valuable in the first place. To set the stage for our discussion I begin this work with an introductory chapter on the nature of ethics, where I have introduced that amount of ethical theory necessary for your work on the specific issues that make up the bulk of this book.

Philosophy is an ongoing process of seeking a deeper understanding of difficult but vital issues to the human condition. As such it seldom arrives at a final word on any subject. This ambiguity is sometimes frustrating to students who desire exact and reliable answers to prob - lems, but wisdom consists not in final dogmatic solutions but in a growing understanding of the issues and considered judgments in favor of one side or the other. As such, I have set forth my best thinking on these life- and- death issues, but I make no pretense to have said anything ap- proaching finality. While I try to present opposing sides of the issue as fairly as possible, I have sometimes made clear where I think the best arguments lead. No doubt you will disagree with some of my reasoning. Fine! My reasoning is offered as a stimulant to get you to think these matters out for yourself and arrive at your own *considered judgments*. But I emphasize that it is a *considered* judgment that must be aimed at, not simply an emotional bias or unexamined intuition. I encourage you to take issue with me, even when you suspect my arguments are sound, to attack these arguments, to improve upon them, and to develop better arguments of your own. For these problems of life and death are your problems. Let the arguments set forth in this book be rungs on a ladder that help you ascend to a higher understanding of the issues, which when reached can be replaced with your own better formulations.

Indeed, I invite you to write me with your responses to my thoughts. I will endeavor to reply.

The intellectual life, that which makes us more than mere animals, is noble and exhilarating. It provides a quality of understanding that is intrinsically good yet can also aid in making life more enjoyable. My wish for you is that applying the intellect to these moral dilemmas will be a worthwhile experience that will excite you to a life of philosophic reflection.

Introduction:
"Doctor Death's" Suicide Machine

Two thousand miles away from her home in Oregon on the afternoon of June 4, 1990, in a 1968 Volkswagen van, Janet Adkins, a vibrant 54-year-old schoolteacher who had been diagnosed as having Alzheimer's disease, pressed the button of a suicide machine and died. A retired 62-year-old pathologist from Royal Oaks, Michigan, Dr. Jack Kevorkian, having been turned away from motels, funeral homes, vacant office space, and even the local Unitarian church, equipped his rusty 1968 Volkswagen van with a cot, clean sheets, and his newly invented suicide machine. The contraption consisted of an intravenous tube and three bottles. One contained a saline solution, another held thiopental sodium to induce sleep, and the third contained potassium chloride, which stops the heart.

Mrs. Adkins had first noticed memory slips and a waning of ability to play her beloved piano and flute some 3 years previously. A year before her death she had been diagnosed as having Alzheimer's disease, an irreversible degeneration of the brain cells that can lead to severe memory loss, dementia, and death. "That just hit her like a bombshell," said her husband, Norman. "Her mind was her life." She had believed for a long time that people had a right to die when life offered greatly diminished quality, and she had joined the Hemlock Society, an organization dedicated to assisting terminally ill people commit suicide.

After experimental treatment failed, she decided to seek a way to end her life. Having consulted with her family and minister, and having received the strong support of her husband, she made inquiries about assisted suicide. Eventually she heard about Dr. Kevorkian's suicide machine. Flying to Michigan, one of the few states where it is not illegal to assist in a suicide, she met Dr. Kevorkian. He spent a few days with Mr. and Mrs. Adkins, monitored the machine inside the van, and notified the police when the ordeal was completed. He had only one regret—that Mrs. Adkins's organs could not be donated because her body remained in the van for several hours before it was removed. "The medical examiner wouldn't let us touch the body," he said.

They were there for 4 hours walking around and scratching their heads. You could have sliced her liver in half and saved two babies and her bone marrow could have been taken, her heart, two kidneys, two lungs, a pancreas. Think of the people that could have been saved. If you were waiting for a new heart, you'd be all for what I'm doing. She had a good strong heart. I know. I watched it on the screen.

The news of Mrs. Adkins's suicide sent earthquake tremors through the nation. *The New York Times* condemned the act and, unsuccessfully, called for Dr. Kevorkian's arrest. Others dubbed him "Dr. Death." Medical ethicists generally were appalled. Susan M. Wolf of the Hastings Center said, "Even the staunchest proponent of physician-assisted suicide should be horrified at this case because there were no procedural protections." Dr. Joanne Lynn of George Washington University said that the claim that Mrs. Adkins's "decision to take her life was made with a clear mind was incompatible with her having Alzheimer's disease." A spokesperson for the American Medical Association announced that this act violated the mutual trust of the doctor–patient relationship. "Our patients should not be concerned that we are going to make a value judgment that their lives are no longer worth living."

Even a representative of the Hemlock Society, the organization dedicated to the cause of voluntary euthanasia, gave only qualified endorsement of Janet Adkins's suicide. "It was unfortunate that Janet Adkins died before she had to die," *The New York Times* reported Cheryl K. Smith, lawyer for the National Hemlock Society, as saying. "She should have been able to wait until it was time to die." If society would only accept voluntary euthanasia for those who have lost all quality of life, Mrs. Adkins could have trusted to others to help her die when she had become incompetent.

Less sympathetically, Dr. John Kiley claimed in the *National Review* that Mrs. Adkins really suffered from a philosophic disorder worse than Alzheimer's disease—a fear of facing the truth. "She was in fatal flight from her terrifying *thought* about Alzheimer's disease. [Dr. Kevorkian] suffers from his own philosophic disease: playing God." The editor went on to say that Mrs. Adkins died "tackily." "The advance promotion for abortion and infanticide imagines them impelled by necessity and performed under ideal conditions. But in time the routine reality becomes sleazier. If life has no intrinsic value, why should the end of life have any grace?"

Fifteen years after the epoch-making Karen Ann Quinlan case America is still wrestling with the question of whether terminally ill patients and others facing greatly diminished quality of life have the right to die. Ironically, it was a machine that assisted Janet Adkins in her death—if Dr. Kevorkian had slipped her the poison directly, he would have been arrested and accused of murder—for it is the very burgeoning of medical technology with its ventilators, artificial hearts, and other machines that can keep people "alive" almost indefinitely. A person may be permanently comatose, persistently vegetative, or without a live cerebral cortex (the brain organ in which resides consciousness and the ability to reason and remember), but legally he or she is still alive—and the mounting doctor and hospital bills prove it.

Is the editor of the *National Review* correct in claiming that people like Mrs. Adkins are moral cowards who cannot face God-given reality? Or that physicians like Dr. Kevorkian are guilty of usurping the authority of God in assisting in suicide? Would such lethal cooperation between physician and patient lead to a confusion of the doctor's role, traditionally one of "promoting life?" Assuming that we grant terminally ill people a right to die, should a new profession be created, "the thanatologist" or "euthanasist," whose function is to assist in suicides? He or she would probably have to be salaried rather than provide "service for fee," lest there be a temptation to solicit patients.

What is the moral difference, if any, between unplugging a respirator and plugging in a suicide machine? Is there a moral difference between purposefully allowing someone to die (when you can easily make a difference) and actively causing that person to die—given the same attitude toward the patient in both instances?

And just what is this idea of sanctity of life that the editorials of both *The New York Times* and the *National Review* cite as the grounds for opposing the suicide machine? Is the *National Review* correct that tacky suicides are related to our views on abortion and represent a loss of faith in the sanctity of life? Is the Roman Catholic Church correct when it says, "A right to death does not exist. Love for life, even a life reduced to a ruin, drives one to protect life with every possible care"?[1] Is life sacred? What does that concept mean in the light of today's technologic labyrinth? Janet Adkins's suicide raises all these questions.

In this book we will be looking at some concrete moral problems, matters of life and death: the idea of sanctity of life, the criteria for death, suicide, euthanasia, abortion, the death penalty, animal rights, and war. The solutions, if there are such, to these problems must be wrested with great effort in the light of the best moral thinking available. All our rational and imaginative powers must be brought to bear on these issues, but the reward in terms of understanding and guidance is worth the toil.

I have tried to present opposite sides of each issue as fairly as possible. Regarding the specific moral problems, I have largely let the flow of the arguments follow their own courses and have not set forth my own views on the matters. For those who are interested in how I come down on these questions, I have written a conclusion, where I spell out some of my views.

I do, however, defend two major theses in this book. The first is that morality is made for humanity, not humanity for morality. That is, moral principles serve for our (and other animals') well-being. Within this general framework, I reject moral relativism and espouse a broadly based moral objectivism. I set forth an overview of the purposes of morality in the first chapter. My second thesis is that the quality-of-life principle should override the sanctity-of-life principle, which, in its absolutist form (as I will argue in the second chapter), is an invalid principle. The quantity of life does not count as much as the quality.

Before we turn to specific moral problems we need to take a look at the nature of morality itself.

Endnote

1. Vatican theologian Gino Concetti, quoted in Joseph and Julia Quinlans' *Karen Ann: The Quinlans Tell Their Story*, with Phyllis Battelle (New York: Doubleday, 1977), p. 211.

Morality and the "Tragedy of the Commons"

What is morality? What is the purpose of moral rules? To answer these questions, let me tell you the story of the "Tragedy of the Commons."

In nineteenth-century England most villages were adjoined by a *commons*, land that was available to all the citizens of a community to use for grazing. If the commons was used judiciously in a small village, individuals could gradually increase their wealth. But as the communities grew the temptation to overgraze grew stronger. The story now known as the "Tragedy of the Commons," first documented by L. Lloyd in the middle of the nineteenth century and fully used in the services of environmental ethics and population policy by Garret Hardin in the 1960s and 1970s, goes like this.[1]

Imagine an unmanaged village commons in which 10 villagers pasture their cattle, each having eight cattle. Since the carrying capacity of the commons is sufficient for 100 cattle, every additional cow put on the commons increases the individual wealth of the farmer without harming anyone. The commons is a source of increased wealth, a blessing to anyone able to use the land's resources without harming anyone. Gradually the farmers grow in wealth, so that each has 10 cows grazing the commons, bringing the total number of cows to 100. Assuming that each cow produces one unit of utility, "utiles," the land is yielding 100 utiles.

Now the land has reached its carrying capacity and it is no longer in the interest of the village to add further cows to the commons. In fact, adding another cow to the land will actually decrease the total utiles, for increased grazing tends to eliminate the sweet green grass on which the cattle feed and ruins the soil by constant trampling. But since the

1

commons is unmanaged it is in the individual farmer's interest to add an additional cow. The entrepreneurial farmer, call him Farmer Brown, who myopically sees short-term advantage for himself but not the long-term welfare of the community, reasons: "It is in my interest to add one more cow beyond the carrying capacity, because if I do this I will be obtaining one more unit of good while paying only a fraction of the negative impact on the land." If the carrying capacity has reached 100 utiles, by adding one more cow he will gain one more utile while diminishing the total utiles of the common by one. The land is worth only 99 utiles. But he gains one whole utile while he shares the one negative unit with nine other farmers, ending up with just under 11 utiles, compared with his neighbors who, instead of the original 10 utiles each, now have 9.9 utiles each.

But, of course, Farmer Jones sees what Brown has done, and he applies the same logic. He adds another cow to the commons, further diminishing the value by two units, the loss of which he shares with the other nine farmers while reaping a positive gain.

Garret Hardin writes of this situation.[2]

> Adding together the component partial utilities, the rational herds-man concludes that the only sensible course for him to pursue is to add another animal to his herd. And another; and another. . . . But this is the conclusion reached by each and every rational herdsman sharing the commons. Each man is *locked in* to a system that compels him to increase his herd without limit . . . in a world that is limited. Ruin is the destination toward which all men rush, each pursuing his own best interest that believes in the freedom of the commons. *Freedom in a commons brings ruin to all.*

This kind of tragedy can be illustrated in many other ways. A few farmers dumping their refuse into a river probably won't affect the river's purity much, but when many companies see this as a cheap way of refuse disposal, the whole region suffers, while each company bears only a fraction of the disadvantage, not enough to offset the money it saves by dumping its waste into the river.

Of course, the "Tragedy of the Commons" is the story of our global environmental catastrophe. A factory saves money by burning a fuel with high sulfur content, but the sulfur dioxide it spews out causes acid rain, which kills a forest or pollutes a lake 1000 miles away—perhaps in a different country. The history of imprudent agricultural practices in North Africa and Spain is responsible for the deserts present there. England was once a land lush with forests, but it unwisely denuded them and now imports its wood from Sweden and other countries.

Hardin's solution is for us to develop mutually agreed upon, mutu-ally coercive rules to save us all from destruction. With growing populations, all wanting to make use of the "commons" of life, we have to limit our consumption and make sure that cheaters don't get away with their theft.

But the lesson of the "Tragedy of Commons" has wider implications for society. It illustrates the role of moral rules in general. Cheating, for example, adds one unit of utility to the cheater but degrades the system so that everyone's work is worth less. Seeing that cheating pays, a second person, who might have been deterred by seeing the first cheater punished, adds her input to the commons, and so the tragedy begins and ruins a good system. A shoplifter steals a few canned goods from the grocery store. If no one else follows suit, not much damage is done, but if others take up the practice, prices are soon driven up to cover for the stolen goods and to pay for security guards and expensive electronic surveillance. We all suffer for pursuing unenlightened self-interest.

The first purpose of morality is to inaugurate a set of agreed upon, coercive, beneficial rules that, if followed, will protect us from harm and allow us to function freely. This negative function keeps society from falling apart, from sinking to a state of chaos where everyone is the enemy of everyone else, where fear and insecurity dominate the mind and prevent peace and happiness. Thomas Hobbes (1588–1679) described this dismal condition as a "state of nature" wherein exists a perpetual war of all against all while life is "solitary, poor, nasty, brutish and short." The purpose of moral rules, first of all, is to prevent the state of nature from occurring. To avoid this condition, we must have rules of justice to resolve conflicts of interest that are mutually agreed upon and seen as just. These rules are primarily negative: do not kill, do not steal, do not break promises, do not cheat, do no unnecessary harm, and the like.

But negative, minimal morality leaves much to be desired, as the tale of Kitty Genovese indicates. In 1964 the United States was stunned by a report from Kew Gardens, Queens, in New York City. A young woman, Kitty Genovese, was brutally stabbed in her neighborhood while 38 respectable, law-abiding citizens watched a killer stalk and stab her in three separate attacks. Her neighbors looked on from their bedroom windows for some 35 minutes as the assailant beat her, stabbed her, left her, and returned to repeat the process two more times until she died. No one lifted a phone to call the police, no one shouted at the criminal, let alone went to Kitty's aid. Finally, a 70-year-old woman called the police. It took them 2 minutes to arrive, but by that time Kitty was dead. Only one other woman came out to testify to what she had witnessed. When the ambulance came an hour later, the whole neighborhood poured out. Asked why they didn't do anything, the responses ranged from "I don't know," and "I was tired," to "Frankly, we were afraid."[3]

None of these witnesses were breaking any laws or any of the negative rules of the minimal moral code. But they were not acting as good citizens either. They should have done something positive on behalf of Kitty Genovese. So we want to add a positive function to morality.

Imagine that you have been miraculously transported to the dark kingdom of Hell, and there you get a glimpse of the suffering of the damned. What is their punishment? Well, they have eternal back itches that ebb and flow constantly. But they cannot scratch their backs, for their arms are paralyzed in a frontal position. And so they writhe with itchiness through eternity. But just as you are beginning to feel the itch in your back, you are suddenly transported to Heaven. What do you see in the kingdom of the blessed? Well, you see people with eternal back itches, who cannot scratch their own backs. But they are all smiling instead of writhing. Why? Because everyone has his or her arms stretched out to scratch someone else's back, and, so arranged in one big circle, a hell is turned into a heaven of ecstasy.

This is positive morality: one big reciprocal back-scratching affair. Note that in Hell no one was breaking any of the moral rules. They simply weren't using reason to transform a hell into heaven.

Full ethical living is in the difference between these two situations, a difference of internalized values. Love versus indifference or hate, alleviating suffering rather than hurting, consistency and justice in the treatment of others and the resolution of conflict. Ethics refers to actions, rules, dispositions, and intentions that promote happiness, ameliorate suffering, and resolve conflicts of interest. Ethical principles are those action-guiding prescriptions that tend to transform a potential hell into a heaven.

The rules are positive, as well as negative, and aim at promoting human flourishing. They enable people to pursue their goals in peace and freedom, encouraging them to friendship and fidelity, challenging them to excellence and a worthwhile life. As it is ingrained in good character, deep morality is a "jewel that shines in its own light." It creates a worthwhile life for its participants and turns a potential hell into something that at its highest point (usually confined to small communities, friendships, and families) approximates a heaven on earth.

ETHICS AS COMPARED WITH RELATED SUBJECTS

The terms *moral* and *ethics* come from Latin and Greek, respectively (*mores* and *ethos*), deriving their meaning from the idea of custom or the fundamental spirit of the culture. I shall follow the custom of using *morality* and *ethics* synonymously to refer to actual or ideal moralities. Sometimes, however, we use the term *ethics* to refer to the philosophic analysis of morality, the systematic endeavor to understand moral concepts and justify moral principles and theories. It analyzes such concepts as "right," "wrong," "permissible," "ought," "good," and "evil" in their moral contexts. Moral philosophy seeks to establish principles of right behavior that may serve as guides to action for individuals and groups. It investigates which values and virtues are paramount to the worthwhile life or worthy society. It builds and scrutinizes arguments in ethical theories, and it seeks to discover valid principles (for example, "Never kill innocent human beings") and the relationship between those principles (for example, does saving a life in some situations constitute a valid reason for breaking a promise?).

Ethics is concerned with values—not what is, but what ought to be. How should I live my life? What is the right thing to do in this situation? Should I always tell the truth? Do I have a duty to report a coworker whom I have seen cheating our company? Should I tell my friend that his spouse is having an affair? Is premarital sex morally permissible? Ought a woman ever to have an abortion? Ethics has a distinct action-guiding aspect and, as such, belongs to the group of practical institutions that includes religion, law, and etiquette.

Ethics may be closely allied to religion, but it need not be. There are both religious and secular ethical systems. Secular or purely philosophical ethics is grounded in reason and common human experience. To use a spatial metaphor, secular ethics is horizontal, lacking a vertical or transcendental dimension. Religious ethics has a vertical dimension, being grounded in revelation or divine authority. These two orientations will often generate different moral principles and standards of evaluation, but they need not. Some versions of religious ethics, which posit God's revelation of the moral law in nature or conscience, hold that reason can discover what is right or wrong even apart from divine revelation.

Ethics is also closely related to law, and in some societies (such as that depicted in the Hebrew Bible or Christian Old Testament) the two are seen as the same single reality. Many laws are instituted to promote well-being, resolve conflicts of interest, and enhance social harmony, just as morality does, but ethics may judge that some laws are immoral without denying that they are valid: for example, laws permitting slavery or irrelevant discrimination against people on the basis of race or sex. A Catholic or antiabortion advocate may believe that the laws permitting abortion are immoral, even invalid, laws.

In a recent television series, "Ethics in America" (PBS, 1989), James Neal, a trial lawyer, was asked what he would do if he discovered that his client had committed a murder some years back for which another man had been convicted and for which that man was going to die in a few days. Mr. Neal said that he had a legal obligation to keep this information confidential and that if he divulged it, he would be disbarred. The question is: Does the attorney in this case have a moral obligation that overrides his legal obligation and that demands he take action to protect the innocent man from being executed? Many would argue that in cases like this, moral reasons override legal rules.

Furthermore, some aspects of morality are not covered by law. For example, while we generally agree that lying is usually immoral, there is no law against it. College newspapers publish advertisements for the sale of phony research papers that students can submit in lieu of their own work. Publication of such ads is legal, but it is not moral. A student's use of such services is clearly immoral. Likewise, Kitty Genovese's neighbors were not guilty of any legal wrongdoing, but surely they were morally culpable for not calling the police or shouting at the assailant.

There is one other major difference between law and morality. In 1351 King Edward of England promulgated a law against treason that made it a crime merely to think homicidal thoughts about the king. But, alas, the law could not be enforced, for no tribunal can search the heart and fathom the intentions of the mind. Other problems arise. If malicious intentions (called in law *mens rea*) were criminally illegal, would we not all deserve imprisonment? Even if it were possible to detect intentions, when should the punishment be administered? As soon as the subject has the intention? But how do we know that the subject will not have a change of mind? Furthermore, is there not a continuum between imagining some harm to X, wishing a harm to X, desiring a harm to X, and intending a harm to X?

While it is impractical to have laws against bad intentions, these intentions are still bad, still morally wrong. Suppose I buy a gun with the intention of killing Uncle Charlie in order to inherit his wealth, but never get a chance to fire it (say, Uncle Charlie moves to Australia). While I have not committed a crime, I have committed a moral wrong.

Finally, law differs from morality in that physical sanctions may enforce the law but only the sanctions of conscience and reputation can enforce morality.

Etiquette also differs from morality in that it concerns the form and style rather than the essence of social existence. Etiquette determines what is polite behavior rather than what is *right* behavior in a deeper sense. It represents society's decision about how we are to dress, greet one another, eat, celebrate festivals, dispose of the dead, and carry out social transactions. Whether we greet each other with a handshake, a bow, a hug, or a kiss on the cheek will vary in different social systems, but none of these rituals has any moral superiority.

People in England hold their fork in their left hand when they eat (and sometimes look at Americans with wonder when they see us holding the fork in our right hand), whereas people in other countries hold it in their right hand or in whichever hand a person feels like holding it, while people in India typically eat without a fork, using the forefingers of their right hand for conveying food from their plate to their mouth.

Although Americans may pride themselves on tolerance and awareness of other cultures, custom and etiquette can be a bone of contention. A friend of mine relates a poignant incident that took place early in his marriage. John and his wife were hosting their first Thanksgiving meal. He had been used to small celebrations with his immediate family, whereas his wife had been used to grand celebrations. He writes, "I had been asked to carve, something I had never done before, but I was willing. I put on an apron, entered the kitchen, attacked the bird with as much artistry as I could muster. And what reward did I get? [My wife] burst into tears. In *her* family the turkey is brought to the *table*, laid before the [father], grace is said, and *then* he carves! 'So I fail patriarchy,' I hollered later. 'What do you expect?'".[4]

Etiquette is a spice of life. Polite manners grace our social existence, but they are not what social existence is about. They help social transactions to flow smoothly, but they are not the substance of those transactions.

At the same time, it can be immoral to offend against etiquette. A cultural crisis recently developed in India when Americans went to the beaches clad in skimpy bikini bathing suits. This was highly offensive to the Indians and an uproar ensued.

There may be nothing intrinsically wrong with wearing skimpy bathing suits in public or with wearing nothing at all, for that matter, but people get used to certain behavioral patterns, and it's terribly insensitive to disregard those customs—especially when you are a guest in someone else's home or country. Not the bathing suits themselves but *insensitivity* is morally offensive.

Law, etiquette, and religion are each important institutions, yet each has limitations. The limitation of the law is that you cannot have a law against every social malady, nor can you enforce every desirable rule. The limitation of etiquette is that is does not get to the heart of what is crucial for personal and social existence. Whether or not one eats with one's fingers pales in significance compared with the importance of being honest, trustworthy, or just. Etiquette is a cultural invention, but morality claims to be a discovery.

The limitation of the religious injunction is that it rests on authority, and we are not always sure of the credentials of the authority, nor of how the authority would rule in ambiguous or new cases. Since most religions are founded on revelation rather than reason, no way exists to convince someone who does not share your religious views that your view is the right one.

Ethics, as the analysis of morality, distinguishes itself from law and etiquette by going deeper into the essence of rational existence. It distinguishes itself from religion by seeking reasons, rather than authority, to justify its principles. Its central purpose is to secure valid principles of conduct and values that can be instrumental in guiding human actions and producing good character. As such it is the most important activity known to humans, for it has to do with how we are to live.

THREE TYPES OF ETHICAL THEORIES

Suppose that you are on an island with a fatally ill millionaire. As she lies dying, she entreats you for one final favor: "I've dedicated my whole life to baseball and have gotten endless pleasure (and some pain) rooting for the New York Yankees for 50 years. Now that I am dying, I want to give all of my assets, $2 million, to the Yankees. Would you take this money [she indicates a box containing the money in large bills] back to New York and give it to the New York Yankees's owner, George Steinbrenner?" You agree to carry out her wish, at which point a huge smile of relief and gratitude breaks out on her face as she expires in your arms. Now on returning to New York you see a newspaper advertisement placed by your favorite World Hunger Relief Organization (whose integrity you do not doubt), pleading for $2 million to be used to save 100,000 people dying of starvation in East Africa. Not only will the $2 million save their lives, but it will be used to purchase appropriate technology and the fertilizers necessary to build a sustainable economy. You reconsider your promise to the dying Yankee fan in the light of this consideration. What should you do with the money?

Or suppose there is a raft floating in the Pacific Ocean with two men who are starving to death. One day they discover some food in an inner compartment of a box on the raft. They have reason to believe that the food will be sufficient to keep one of them alive until the raft reaches an island where help is available, but they believe if they share the food both of them will most likely die. Now one of these men is a brilliant scientist who has the cure for cancer in his mind. The other man is undistinguished. Otherwise there is no relevant difference between the two men. What is the morally right thing to do? Share the food and hope against the odds for a miracle? Flip a coin to see which man gets the food? Give the food to the scientist?

What is the right thing to do in these kinds of situations? Take some traditional moral principles and see if they help you come to a decision. One principle often given to guide action is "Let your conscience be your guide." I recall this principle with fondness, for it was the one my father taught me at an early age, and it still echoes in my mind. But does it help here? No, since conscience is primarily a function of our upbringing and will speak to people in different ways according to how they were brought up. Depending on upbringing, some people feel no qualms of conscience about terrorist acts, while others feel the torments of conscience over stepping on a gnat. Suppose that your conscience tells you to give the money to the Yankees while my conscience tells me to give the money to the World Hunger Organization. How can we even discuss the choices? If conscience is the end of the matter, we're left mute.

Another principle urged on us is "Do whatever is most loving." St. Augustine (354–430) said, "Love God and do whatever you want." Love is surely a wonderful value, but is it enough to guide our actions when there is a conflict of interest? "Love is blind," it has been said, "but reason like marriage is an eye opener." Whom should I love in the case of the dispersement of the millionaire's money?—the millionaire or the starving people? How do I apply the principle of love in the case of the two starving men on the raft? Should I take into consideration the needs of the two men, their families, those in need of a cure for cancer, or everyone? It's not clear how love alone will settle anything. In fact it is not obvious that we must always do what is most loving. Should we always treat our enemies in loving ways? Or is it morally acceptable to hate those who have purposefully and unjustly harmed us, our loved ones, and other innocent people? Should the survivors of Auschwitz love Hitler? I can't see that they should. Repentance is a necessary condition for forgiveness. Love alone does not solve difficult moral issues. Reason is also needed.

A third principle often given to guide us in moral actions is the Golden Rule, "Do unto others as you would have them do unto you." This is also a noble rule of thumb, which works in simple common-sense situations, but it has problems. First of all, it cannot be taken literally. Suppose I love to hear loud rock music. I would love for you to play it loudly for me. So I reason that I should play it loudly for you—even though I know that you hate the stuff. So the rule must be modified, "Do unto others as you would have them do unto you if you were in their shoes." But this still has problems. If I were in the shoes of Sirhan Sirhan (the assassin of Robert Kennedy), I'd want to be released from the penitentiary, but it's not clear that he should be. If I put myself in a sex-starved person's shoes, I'd want the next available person of the opposite sex to have sex with me, but it's absurd to suppose that I have a duty to submit myself to someone's present desire to have sex with me.

Likewise, the Golden Rule doesn't tell us to whom we should give the millionaire's money or the food on the life raft.

Conscience, love, and the Golden Rule are worthy rules of thumb to help us through life. They work for most of us most of the time with ordinary moral situations. But in more complicated cases, especially where there are legitimate conflicts of interests, they are too limited.

A more promising strategy for solving dilemmas is that of following moral rules. Suppose that you decided to give the millionaire's money to the Yankees to keep your promise or because to do otherwise would be stealing. The principle you followed would be "Always keep your promise" or " Thou shalt not steal" (the Eighth Commandment of the Bible). Principles are valuable in life. All learning involves understanding a set of rules. As the philosopher R. M. Hare says, " To learn to do anything is never to learn to do an individual act; it is always to learn to do acts of a certain kind in a certain kind of situation; and this is to learn a principle. . . . Without principles we could not learn anything whatever from our elders. . . . Every generation would have to start from scratch and teach itself. But . . . self-teaching, like all other teaching, is the teaching of principles."[5]

In the case of the millionaire's money if you decided to act on the principle of promise-keeping or not stealing, or if you decided on the basis of the principle of fairness or equal justice to share the food in the case of the two men on the raft, then you adhere to a type of moral theory called *deontology*. Perhaps you agree with the greatest deontologist in the history of moral philosophy, Immanuel Kant (1724–1804), and chose the principle of keeping your promises (or not stealing) and sharing equally since they seemed like reasonable universal laws. We could will that everyone follow these principles. Furthermore, you might reason, the end never justifies the means, so I ought not help people by stealing from other people.

If, on the other hand, you decided to give the money to the World Hunger Relief Organization to save an enormous number of lives and restore economic solvency to the region, you sided with a type of theory called *teleology* or teleologic ethics. Likewise, if you decided to give the food to the scientist because he would probably do more good with his life, you sided with the teleologist.

Traditionally, two major types of ethical systems have dominated the field, one in which the locus of value is the *act* or kind of act (or intention behind the act), the other in which the locus of value is the outcome or *consequences* of the act. The act-type of theory is called *deontological* (from the Greek *deon*, which means "duty," and *logos*, meaning "logic") and the consequence theory is called *teleological* (from the Greek *telos*, which means "end" or "result"). For teleologic ethics the end always justifies the means. For deontologic ethics the end never justifies the means; the morality of means and ends is not connected. Some acts are intrinsically right or wrong, regardless of their consequences. Hence their consequences do not determine whether they ought to be done.

A teleologist is a person whose ethical decision making aims solely at maximizing such goods as pleasure, happiness, and welfare, while minimizing such evils as pain and suffering. Thus, for the teleologist the standard of right or wrong action is the comparative consequences of the available actions. That act is right which produces the best consequences. Whereas the deontologist is concerned only with the rightness of the act itself, the teleologist asserts that there is no such thing as an act having intrinsic worth. Only happiness or well-being has intrinsic worth. While for the deontologist there is something intrinsically bad about lying, the only thing wrong with lying for the teleologist is the bad consequences it produces. If you can reasonably calculate that a lie will do even slightly more good than telling the truth, you have an obligation to lie.

The main type of teleologic ethics is utilitarianism, a theory that urges us to do the act that is likely to bring about "the greatest good for the greatest number." Utilitarianism began with the work of Scottish philosophers Frances Hutcheson (1694–1746), David Hume (1711–1776), and Adam Smith (1723–1790), and came into its classic stage in the persons of English social reformers Jeremy Bentham (1748–1832) and John Stuart Mill (1806–1873). These British philosophers were the nonreligious ancestors of the twentieth-century secular humanists, optimistic about human nature and our ability to solve our problems without recourse to providential grace. Engaged in a struggle for legal as well as moral reform, they were impatient with the rule-bound character of law and morality in eighteenth- and nineteenth-century Great Britain and tried, quite successfully, to make the law serve human needs and interests.

But there is a third type of moral theory, one going back to Thomas Hobbes, which is reflected in our discussion of the tragedy of the commons. This type is called *contractualism* and emphasizes the aspect of resolving conflicts of interest in a potentially destructive situation ("a state of nature" where life is a "war of all against all"). While contractualists usually emphasize the negative aspects of morality and therefore are minimalists, they are not necessarily so. We can have positive agreements of mutual help as well as negative agreements such as a mutual nonaggression pact that is so basic for the commonweal. The point is that whereas the other two systems use reason to set forth universal prescriptions ("Do not kill anyone" or "Do what will maximize utility"), contractualism depends on agreements made or implied by people that can be *enforced,* for as Hobbes noted, "Covenants without swords are mere words and of no strength to secure a man at all."[6]

In the case of the millionaire, her death and lack of a written, enforceable will or agreement absolves the contractualist of any obligation to give the money to the New York Yankees, but the contractualist has no agreement with the starving people of East Africa either. He may keep the money. He does no wrong according to contractualist principles. Similarly, there is no preordained rule to guide the two men on the raft. They are free to come to any agreement they like—flip a coin, fight it out, or share the food. There is no right or wrong before the agreement, although some courses of action are more rational than others in terms of promoting long-term self-interest. And rational self-interest is precisely what the contractualist tries to promote.

The contractualist need not be a crass egoist. He or she may happen to value friends, family, or nation very highly, in which case it makes sense to promote the welfare of friends, family, or nation. But human nature being what it is, the self will probably loom large in any decision making, so that the contractualist will typically negotiate agreements that will best serve his or her long-term interests.

Each of these three theories has strengths and weaknesses. The strength of deontologic ethics is that it promotes ideal universalizable rules that seem impartial and reasonable. The strength of utilitarianism is that it aims directly at promoting human happiness, using rules only as means to that end. The strength of contractualism is that it provides motivation for carrying out the moral rules—they are clearly in your interest, as long as everyone adheres to them and adequate sanctions back them up.

The weakness of deontologic ethics is that the rules sometimes get in the way of promoting human happiness (sometimes justice fails to maximize happiness). The weakness of utilitarianism is that it sometimes sacrifices justice to utility (for example, it sacrifices the innocent for the greater good of society). Both deontologic and utilitarian ethics have difficulty explaining why we should always be moral—even when it is not in our interest (for example, I could successfully cheat and come out richer or happier). The weakness of contractualism is that it sacrifices universal ideals, such as a duty to feed the poor or help people with whom we have no contract. Why should we even save the environment for posterity? What has posterity ever done for us? Contractualism easily deteriorates into selfishness. Furthermore, unless the contractors are self-disciplined, they need a leviathan police force to enforce the social contract.

None of these theories is without problems. Perhaps each has a role in a full moral system, but you will probably incline to one type of theory more than the others. Perhaps you will want to combine features of different theories to work out a synthesis of two or more of them. One suggestion is the following. Suppose we recognize that deontologic and teleologic ethics each has a valid insight. The insight of deontologic ethics is that we ought to promote *justice*, treating each person fairly, with equal consideration, and so forth. The insight of teleologic ethics is that morality has been made for humans (and perhaps other creatures), so that we have a duty to promote *happiness*—call this the principle of benevolence. Happily, most of the time these two principles will not conflict, so that when we keep our promises, we will be both acting justly and promoting happiness. However, sometimes we will enter situations like the ones described in this chapter where justice and the promotion of happiness conflict. If I keep my promise to the millionaire (that is, act justly), I will give her money to the Yankees. If I act on the principle of promoting the most happiness, I will break my promise and give the money to those whose lives depend on charity. Here one must decide which principle has priority, benevolence or justice. There are reasons to support each side in this debate, but in the end the individual must make up his or her own mind on the matter.

The lesson to be drawn is this. While objective moral principles exist that are justified by the nature of personhood and the nature of society, there are situations where our principles conflict, so that it is not clear which valid principle should override the other. Sometimes further reasoning or community discussion will help you decide the matter, but at other times dilemmas are so difficult that you have to admit that you don't know the answer. At times when we have done our best and see two courses of action as equally justified, either is permissible. In these cases we are allowed to follow our intuitions, take a vote, or simply flip a coin.

But not all of life is so problematic. Clear thinking about principles will guide us to reasonable solutions in most of life's moral problems. Making sure that we have all the facts available, that we understand the issues, and that we have worked out our moral theory are the best preparations for knowing how we should act. But we never finish working out the finer details of our theory or understand all the factors important in life's situations. The moral enterprise is a neverending but vitally important process.

Much more needs to be said on the matter of working out your own moral theory. If you would like to pursue the matter further, several books are listed in the bibliography at the end of this book. In several places we will note how the different moral theories resolve the problems discussed in this book.

Study Questions

1. What is morality and why is it important for a society to have moral rules?

2. Discuss the significance of the "Tragedy of the Commons." What lessons does it teach us? Can you think of applications of the metaphor in daily life?

3. What is the difference between a moral principle, a legal rule, a principle of etiquette, an aesthetic judgment, and a religious principle? Do these different types of principles overlap? For example, can some behavior be so aesthetically repulsive as to be morally wrong? On the other hand, just because I am repulsed by your behavior, is it wrong?

4. Discuss the differences between the three classic moral theories, deontologic ethics, utilitarianism, and contractualism. What are the strengths and weaknesses of each? Can they be combined to overcome individual weaknesses?

5. Many people hold that the Golden Rule or the Principle of Love is sufficient for ethical decisions. What are the problems with viewing ethics in this manner?

6. Are moral principles absolutely binding or are they valid relative to culture? That is, are any moral principles universal or do all principles depend on social approval?

7. If all principles are valid relative to culture (a view we call *ethical relativism*), the following may be considered. My friends and I believe in cheating on class tests. But such cheating is not socially approved, so it is wrong, But can we not form our own subculture (like a fraternity or sorority) to make cheating morally permissible?

8. You have just discovered that your best friend's wife is having an affair. Should you tell your friend and risk ruining the marriage, should you approach the wife and urge her to dissolve the affair, or should you do nothing? Do you have any moral duty here?

Endnotes

1. Garret Hardin, "The Tragedy of the Commons," *Science* 162 (1968), 1243– 48.

2. Ibid.

3. Martin Gansberg, "138 Who Saw Murder Didn't Call Police," *The New York Times*, March 27, 1964.

4. From John Buehrens and Forrester Church, *Our Chosen Faith* (Boston: Beacon Press, 1989), p. 140.

5. R. M. Hare, *Language of Morals* (Oxford University Press, 1952), pp. 60f.

6. In discussing contractualism I am referring to *actual types* of contractualism, such as Hobbes's *Leviathan* (1651), Gilbert Harman's "A Defense of Moral Relativism" (*Philosophical Review*, 1976), and David Gauthier's *Morals By Agreement* (1986), rather than *ideal types* such as John Rawls's *A Theory of Justice* (1971). Rawls's system is a *hypothetical* or *ideal* type of contractualism that posits the kinds of contract we would agree to under special conditions, such as if we didn't know what sort of aptitudes we had or what our sex, race, or social class was. Ideal contractual systems tend to approximate either deontologic or utilitarian systems.

CHAPTER 2

The Sanctity of Life versus the Quality of Life

The fundamental fact of human awareness is this: "I am life that wants to live in the midst of other life that wants to live." A thinking man feels compelled to approach all life with the same reverence he has for his own.

—ALBERT SCHWEITZER[1]

Sanctity of life is not just a vague theological precept. It is the foundation of a free society.

—NORMAN CANTOR[2]

Imagine that we invented a mighty Convenience Machine that would make our lives wonderfully more enjoyable and enable us to reach more of our goals. Unfortunately, using the machine would cost us about 50,000 lives each year. Would you use the machine? Should we allow it to be sold on the market? When I have asked audiences this question, there is virtually universal agreement that we should not, for no amount of comfort equals the value of a single life. Human life is of absolute value. "Life is sacred."

We are often told that we ought not to take life because it is sacred. This statement is frequently used as the major premise in arguments opposing abortion, suicide, euthanasia, war, and the death penalty. Sometimes it is used to promote animal rights or vegetarianism. With the onset of sophisticated medical technology, which can keep a person in a persistent vegetative state alive indefinitely, the question of the sanctity of life becomes especially urgent. Does a physician have an absolute duty to sustain indefinitely the life of an irreversibly comatose patient by means of expensive life support systems while resources are denied poor families? Must defective newborns, no matter how degrading or painful their condition, be kept alive and cared for? Should all fetuses, no matter how burdensome for the mother, the family, or society, be given an absolute right to life, so that abortion is equated with murder?

Life is wonderful! The sprouting of a plant, the blooming of a flower, the emergence of a chick from an egg, the birth of a baby—who could not stand in wonder at these miracles? The mystery of life is the ultimate miracle, one that must have amazed the cave man millennia ago as much as it does us today. Even those with little religious feeling stand in awe of the birthing process and are likely to believe that birth is a gift of God and that only God should be able to end one's life. Murder is universally condemned as the worst crime of all.

There is a primordial tendency to treat life as sacred, to surround life with a mystic aura and set high value to it. Edward Shils suggests that it is a universal, self-evident intuition that even predates organized religion. It is the "proto-religious" feeling. Thus it is not surprising that virtually every major religion has espoused a version of the sanctity of life. Indeed, the idea of the sanctity of life is essentially a religious one. Its roots are in a religious world view. Animists believe that all things have souls and are to be revered. Vitalists believe that all biologic life contains a dynamic force that cannot be reduced to the elements of chemistry or physics. Hindus and Jains believe all animals have a divine soul; Jews and Christians believe only humans have sacred souls. Each person is endowed with an immortal soul that is of infinite value. It is our true self and that which gives us whatever worth we have. Questions do remain of whether such a thing as a soul exists, of what evidence is available for the existence of such an entity, and who, if anyone, possesses a soul.

We will examine two versions of the sanctity of life principle in this chapter—the vitalist version and the humanist version. The vitalist version says that all living things are sacred and to be revered. The humanist version says that human life is special, only human life is infinitely valuable.

VITALISM

Albert Schweitzer (1875–1965), the famous missionary doctor and Nobel Peace Prize winner, combined a Christian and animist view of life in advocating a vitalism that he called "Reverence for Life." While serving as a doctor in French Equatorial Africa, Schweitzer's personal goal was to discover a universal ethical principle. One day in 1915 while wearily trekking along an island set in the middle of a wide river, he spotted four hippopotamuses and their young plodding along on the other side of the island. "Just then, in my great tiredness and discouragement, the phrase

'Reverence for Life' struck me like a flash. As far as I knew, it was a phrase I had never heard nor ever read. I realized at once that it carried within itself the solution to the problem that had been torturing me." In a passage that has become a classic expression of the Sanctity of Life principle Schweitzer explains what he means by the "Reverence for Life"[3]:

> I am life which wills to live, and I exist in the midst of life which wills to live. . . . A living world—and life view, informing all the facts of life, gushes forth from it continually, as from an eternal spring. A mystically ethical oneness with existence grows forth from it unceasingly. . . . Ethics thus consists in this, that I experience the necessity of practising the same reverence for life toward all will-to-live, as toward my own. Therein [lies] the fundamental principle of morality. It is *good* to maintain and cherish life; it is *evil* to destroy and to check life. A man is really ethical only when he obeys the constraint laid on him to help all life which he is able to succour, and when he goes out of his way to avoid injuring anything living. He does not ask how far this or that life deserves sympathy as valuable in itself, nor how far it is capable of feeling. To him life as such is sacred. He shatters no ice crystal that sparkles in the sun, tears no leaf from its tree, breaks off no flower, and is careful not to crush any insect as he walks. If he works by lamplight on a summer evening, he prefers to keep the window shut and to breathe stifling air, rather than to see insect after insect fall on his table with singed and sinking wings. . . . Should he pass by an insect which has fallen into a pool, he spares the time to reach it a leaf or stalk on which it may clamber and save itself.
>
> Ethics is in its unqualified form extended responsibility with regard to everything that has life.

Schweitzer ordered his life according to this principle. Instead of choosing the comfort of a cool breeze in his rooms in hot Equatorial Africa, he kept the windows shut so as not to attract insects and flies who would otherwise have immolated themselves against the kerosene lamps or hot light bulbs.

Schweitzer's Reverence for Life principle has been heralded as the essence of morality, a recognition of our symbiotic relationship with nature, a benevolence to all living things, a harbinger of heaven. Is it true?

In this passage Schweitzer has gone beyond the idea that all life is sacred to include inanimate things such as ice crystals as part of the moral domain. But ignoring this problem and concentrating on his vitalism, one wonders if he ever weeded his garden or exterminated termites. Did he ever use bacteria-killing antibiotics to help cure his sick patients? According to Schweitzer's principle, all of life is equally sacred, so that we may not choose between saving the life of a phytoplankton or a mosquito, on the one hand, and saving that of a human being, on the other hand. If life is the only relevant consideration and questions of quality do not enter in, two cockroaches are worth more than one human being. The more living things, the better, regardless of levels of sentience or consciousness.

Note that adherents of the Sanctity of Life principle may display apparent inconsistency in their behavior. An animist may pull weeds from his or her garden or cut down a tree to build a house, a Hindu may kill an animal to save a human life. Even Schweitzer performed operations in which millions of live bacteria were sacrificed for the health of one human.

Many will find this leveling of life forms highly implausible. Since the vitalist does not offer an argument for this absolute position but only an intuition, it is left to anyone who fails to have that intuition to reject such absolutism. We may agree that life is valuable without agreeing that it is the one and only absolute value.

SACRED HUMANISM

The *sacred* is a religious idea. God (or the gods) is holy and whatever else is holy derives its holiness from God. While religious vitalists like Schweitzer believe that all life is holy, Jews and Christians believe that only humans have sacred souls. Since God created humans in His own image, all humans are equally and essentially valuable, though they may lose merit through sin and acquire merit by improving the character of their souls. But, even as a bent and corroded coin bears the king's image, so the most distorted and degraded human life still bears the sacred image of the King of kings.

"Thou has made man a little lower than the angels, as little gods," the Psalmist writes. "According to Jewish law," writes Rabbi Byron Sherwin, "life is to be preserved, even at great cost. Each moment of human life is considered intrinsically sacred. Preserving life supersedes living the 'good life'. The sacredness of life and the uniqueness of the individual require that every possible action be taken to preserve life."[4] The eminent Protestant ethicist Paul Ramsey expresses the Christian perspective this way.[5]

> The value of a human life is ultimately grounded in the value God is placing on it. . . . Man is a sacredness *in* human biological processes no less than he is a sacredness in the human social or political order. . . . Every human being is a unique, unrepeatable opportunity to praise God. His life is entirely an ordination, a loan, and a steward-

ship. His essence is his existence before God and to God, as it is from Him. His dignity is 'an alien dignity,' an evaluation that is not of him but placed upon him by the divine decree.

There are two central questions that we must ask with regard to the doctrine of the sanctity of life. The first is: What are the implications of the doctrine? If all human life is equally sacred, would it mean that we should become vegetarians and even forgo using antibiotics? The second question is: What is the evidence for the Sanctity of Human Life principle? If you give up the religious basis of the doctrine, can you continue to maintain the doctrine on some other grounds?

Let us turn to the first question. The doctrine of the sanctity of human life seems to provide a basis for the pro-life movement. If all *Homo sapiens* are possessed with eternal and sacred souls and if fetuses are *Homo sapiens*, then abortion is murder. Likewise, all humans, whether severely deformed, retarded, or in agony have something sacred within, so that it would be immoral to shorten their lives.

Rabbi Moshe Tendler puts it this way: "Human life is of infinite value. This in turn means that a piece of infinity is also infinity and a person who has but a few moments to live is no less of value than a person who has 60 years to live . . . a handicapped individual is a perfect specimen when viewed in an ethical context. The value is an absolute value. It is not relative to life expectancy, to state of health, or to usefulness to society."[6]

As an example of how radical the Sanctity of Human Life principle is, note the following case described by Anthony Shaw[7]:

A baby was born with Down's syndrome (mongolism), intestinal obstruction, and a congenital heart condition. The mother, believing that the retarded infant would be impossible for her to care for adequately, refused to consent to surgery to remove the intestinal obstruction. Without surgery, of course, the baby would soon die. Thereupon a local child-welfare agency, invoking a state child-abuse statute, obtained a court order directing that surgery be performed. After a complicated course of surgery and thousands of dollars worth of medical care, the infant was returned to her mother. In addition to her mental retardation, the baby's physical growth and development remained markedly retarded because of her severe cardiac disease. A follow up enquiry eighteen months after the baby's birth revealed that the mother felt more than ever that she had been done an injustice.

Many of us would object to this treatment. It seems unjust to force an infant with such low quality of life expectations onto a family, but those holding to the Sanctity of Life principle would reply that we are not to play God in deciding who is to live.

As Paul Ramsey says in rejecting the possibility of abortion in the case of a fetus with Tay–Sachs disease, "There is no reason for saying that [6 months in the life of a baby born with the invariably fatal Tay–Sachs disease] are a life span of lesser worth to God than living seventy years before the onset of irreversible degeneration. . . . All our days and years are of equal worth whatever the consequences; death is not more a tragedy at one time than another."[8]

Quality of life considerations are irrelevant to theologians like Tendler and Ramsey, as they were to the Department of Health and Human Services in inaugurating "Baby Doe" regulations. "Considerations such as anticipated or actual limited potential of an individual . . . are irrelevant and must not determine the decisions concerning medical care."[9]

The question is, why don't those who treat human life as an absolute stop driving cars? If you drive a car, your behavior shows that you don't value human life as absolute. Indeed, the Convenience Machine in our earlier thought experiment is the car. We know with high probability that each year over 50,000 people will lose their lives in automobile accidents in the United States alone. The car also causes harmful air pollution, which shortens life. As I write these words the United States is engaged in a destructive war in the Middle East over oil, 40 percent of which is consumed by automobiles. Anyone who believes that human life really is of absolute value should be against the use of the automobile! And yet the staunchest right-to-lifer drives to the antiabortion protest without blinking a eye over the inconsistency, and the most militant pacifist and abolitionist (with regard to capital punishment) has not the slightest conscience qualm when it comes to gunning his or her Cadillac, Ford, or Nissan.

Of course, we could reinterpret the notion of the sanctity of life in such a way as to make it less radical, a nonabsolute. We could interpret it as offering a presumption in favor of preserving life wherever possible unless a strong moral reason overrode it. But then the principle would lose much of its force as quality of life considerations become relevant.

Here the most pressing question arises: Is the Sanctity of Life principle true? As we saw earlier, the principle rests on a religious foundation, and different religions generate different conclusions as to the nature of this sanctity idea. So one problem for us to settle is whether any religion is the true religion. Does any religion possess credentials to claim our rational allegiance? This is not a question we can take up here, except to say that liberal versions of Judaism and Christianity do allow for quality of life considerations.

One thing more should be said. The notion of a separate soul inhabiting a body, so important for the absolutist view of the Sanctity of Life doctrine, has lost much of its credibility in the light of neuroscience. According to neuroscience, the brain, not a separate soul, is the center of mental activity, the locus of memories, and the place where consciousness, an emergent property of the nervous system, resides. If this is so, we can suppose that when the brain dies, the person dies.

This is no proof that there is no soul, but neuroscience puts the matter in doubt. Furthermore, those who doubt whether there is a God will doubt even more whether animals or humans have god-like souls.

Can the Sanctity of Life principle survive without a religious basis? How could it? If no transcendent dimension ("the holy") exists, how can individual things be sacred? The doctrine loses its essential support.

THE QUALITY OF LIFE

The doctrine of the sanctity of life is opposed by the doctrine of the quality of life. The Quality of Life principle states that the values a life contains are more important than mere living. Some kinds of life are more worth living than others. Socrates said, "The unexamined life is not worth living," suggesting that a life of reflection and moral deliberation is a worthwhile life. While life is the foundation of values, without these other values life is not worth living. Life by itself has only *potential value* depending on these other features.

We may represent the difference between the sanctity of life view and the quality of life view this way. Whereas the sanctity of life view looks at nonbeing as a negative and at even the worst human existence as a positive (small though it may be), the quality of life view looks at nonbeing as neutral and regards some lives as having positive value and others as having negative value. Deeply moral people, productive geniuses who advance our knowledge, such as Newton and Einstein, and decent people all have various degrees of positive worth, whereas evil people or people whose lives are plagued with suffering and unremitting agonizing pain may have negative worth. We may represent the scorecard this way.

	Quality of Life Position	*Sanctity of Life Position*
The optimally good life	+1	+1
Nonbeing (not being born)	0	−1
The maximal bad life	−1	+0.01 (or $n > 0$)

The two positions differ radically on the status of not being born (or more accurately, never having become conscious) and being born to a bad life. For those who hold a sanctity of life view not to live is tragic—the more life the better. It's as though souls are waiting to be born and who will not inhabit heaven unless we do our duty to procreate as much and as often as possible. The quality of life view holds that we cannot give any value to what never even exists. Likewise, for the sanctity of life view even a horrible life with gratuitous suffering is good, whereas for the quality of life view some lives have negative value.

The truth is that Judaism and Christianity are ambiguous on this issue. They sometimes speak as though life were an absolute or near absolute value. But they also contain quality of life aspects that qualify the high value of life. Quality counts to some degree. Even Jesus, usually seen as the paragon of respect for life, said of Judas, "It were better that he were never born." (Matt 26:24), suggesting that nonexistence is preferable to an evil existence. An evil life has negative worth; it is bad. Evil is associated with causing gratuitous suffering and pain, with doing those things harmful to others. Hence, we might conclude that even from a Christian perspective death is preferable to excruciating pain without the expectation of remission. Furthermore, if life were an absolute, then God would have no right to call on believers to risk their lives for their religion.

There is further evidence that the Judeo-Christian position has never really regarded life as an absolute value. Risks of life are often worth the goals of enhancing the quality of life for others. The martyr, the missionary to hostile territory, the settler, the witness to the truth all value something higher than their own life. If biologic lives were all-important, we should not wash ourselves or brush our teeth, for in doing so we unnecessarily kill millions of human cells with the exact genetic information of a single-cell zygote!

Just how the Quality of Life principle operates is a controversial matter. Let's look at how typical representatives of the three ethical theories discussed in the last chapter view the matter. Take first the classic deontologist, Immanuel Kant (1724–1804), himself a liberal Christian. Kant reinterpreted the idea of the sanctity of human life in such a way as to make it dependent on a determinate quality: rationality. It is our ability to engage in rational deliberation that gives us worth. Kant wrote,[10]

> Now I say, man, and in general every rational being exists as an end in himself and not merely as a means to be arbitrarily used by this or that will. . . . Act so that you treat humanity, whether in your own person or in that of another, always as an end and never as a means only. Human beings qua rational have an inherent dignity and so ought to treat each other as ends and never merely as means.

We are to respect human beings and all rational beings simply because they are *persons* (a technical term, standing for the possession of the requisite value-endowing properties) capable of moral self-determination. Social status, wealth, talents, education, intelligence, occupation, and other qualities are unimportant.

Kant's position has frequently been analyzed to mean that rational self-consciousness is the distinguishing feature of human worth. As such the severely retarded, senile, and insane are not really persons since they do not possess self-conscious rationality. On this criterion fetuses and infants are also nonpersons, though they are potential persons. On the other hand, adult chimpanzees, dolphins, whales, and other animals probably are persons, since they manifest behavior similar to self-conscious humans.

There are many ways of interpreting Kant's notion of the kingdom of ends. One interpretation leads us to do whatever we can to preserve all rational creatures, so that suicide and driving automobiles would be morally forbidden. Another way of interpreting Kant is to emphasize the rational independence of persons, their *autonomy*. Never exploit or impose your values on other persons, since they, qua rational, must be left to decide for themselves on how they should live their life. In this case, Kant's principle would justify suicide when life irretrievably loses its meaning.

Kant's idea that reason gives us worth can be questioned. Some have called it the idolization of reason. If following rules and exercising deductive reasoning count, computers can reason, and robots may have artificial intelligence, but there is nothing intrinsically valuable about them. It's not wrong to discard your old computer when you can get a better one, but it is wrong to discard your aging parent or spouse even when you can find a more rational one.

Another problem in Kant's formula of rationality is that it seems to lead not to equal human worth but to unequal worth, for if rational self-consciousness gives us our value, then the fact that some people are more self-aware and rational should lead us to conclude that these people are worth more than those who are less self-aware or rational. Kant and his followers would reply that rational self-consciousness is a threshhold concept. As long as you have some of that property, you are of equal value. But this is just pious bootstrapping, a desperate move to save a secular faith in equality. A convincing explanation for equal human worth based on unequal rationality has yet to be offered. The appeal to reason as the criterion of intrinsic value is essentially inegalitarian.

The idea of what makes humans valuable is problematic. Kant's insight that the locus of human value is rational self-consciousness is persuasive because it enables us to have plans and projects, to project our wishes into the future, to discipline ourselves so that we sacrifice immediate pleasure for future good, and to develop language and communicate with one another.

Reason alone is not enough to give us a right to life, since computers can think. What gives our reason a special worth is the fact that we are persons who can feel pains and emotions, that we have a sense of identity that computers lack (at least up until now). That is, we have the combination of self-consciousness and rationality that makes us intrinsically valuable and grants us a right to life.

The defective neonate described above by Anthony Shaw would be allowed to die on a Kantian view, but a normal fetus would not be allowed to be aborted, since it would likely develop into a rational child.

Utilitarians like Jeremy Bentham (1748–1832), John Stuart Mill (1806–1873), and Peter Singer find quality of life in the notion of happiness, including the minimization of suffering. Pleasure or happiness is equated with the good and pain and suffering with evil. The aim of utilitarianism is to maximize happiness and minimize suffering and pain. The ability to enjoy things and to suffer—not reason—grants every sentient being, animals and humans, moral consideration. So when our life becomes too frought with pain or suffering, we have reason to take our life.

Utilitarians would encourage the death of the defective neonate as a means to alleviate suffering in others (where a quality of life is extremely unlikely). Utilitarians are inclined to support prochoice organizations like Planned Parenthood and the National Abortion Rights Action League since therapeutic abortions can be justified on utilitarian grounds.

The accusation that utilitarians sometimes play God, and take life into their own hands, is a charge that they need to answer. On the one hand, they point out that all medical decisions of whether to treat sick people (thus thwarting *natural* processes) are in a sense playing God. On the other hand, with regard to situations in which innocents may be sacrificed for the good of the whole, their thinking tends to become more complicated and qualified. Some utilitarians, called *rule-utilitarians*, urge only that we devise a set of rules that would result in the greatest good for society. These thinkers would reject most proposals for sacrificing innocent lives for the good of the whole.

Finally, contractualists like Thomas Hobbes (1588–1679) would argue that the notion of intrinsic human worth is a mistake. Since all value is a function of human desires, the only value a person has is his or her market value, how much he or she is valued by others. My children have a value because I desire that they live and prosper.

According to this kind of contractualist, we don't need a notion of inherent human value to live moral lives, for all morality consists in agreements that we make with others or with society as a whole. We all accept a mutual nonaggression pact, agree to keep contracts, submit to the law, and the like. If we examine the situation carefully and choose to allow abortions or voluntary euthanasia, there is nothing more that can be said.

Many regard contractual ethics as having a serious weakness in being willing to undermine "minority rights." If the social contract we embrace fails to include certain powerless people, the contractualists on their principles are guilty of no mistake. Deontologists and most utilitarians object, but they must explain why contractualism is wrong. If we give up the religious notion of the sanctity of human life, are we left with nothing more than a degrading contractualism?

Some people argue that if we give up the idea of the sanctity of human life, we will be on the slippery slope to Auschwitz. Let us see how slippery slope arguments might be used to support the notion that human life is of absolute value, never to be taken under any circumstances (except possibly to save one's own life). The argument is that once we admit that human life may be taken, considerations other than the value of human life can be considered to override a right to life. The danger is that utilitarian considerations will outweigh the right to life so that a situation such as developed in Nazi Germany could arise. Witness these excerpts from letters sent by the German chemical company I. G. Farben to the commander at Auschwitz during the Second World War.

> In contemplation of experiments with a new soporific drug, we would appreciate your procuring for us a number of women. . . . We received your answer but consider the price of 200 marks a woman excessive. We propose to pay not more than 170 marks a head. If agreeable, we will take possession of the women. We need approximately 150.

After the women were received by I. G. Farben and the experiments accomplished, a second letter was sent by the chemical company: "Received the order of 150 women. Despite their emaciated condition, they were found satisfactory. We shall keep you posted on developments concerning this experiment. . . . The tests were made. All subjects died. We shall contact you shortly on the subject of a new load."[11]

The letters show to what depths of evil people can descend. Yet you do not have to believe in the Sanctity of Life principle, which is an extreme notion, to hold that the Nazi practices of sacrificing humans was reprehensible. If what we have said about the Quality of Life principle is accurate, it is sufficient to prohibit such atrocious conduct. Whether in a deontologic or utilitarian guise, the Quality of Life view is that human beings are valuable by virtue of their rational self-consciousness or capacity for happiness and that their right to life may not be violated. It does not deny that life is important, simply that it is sufficient in itself to procure any positive value.

The Quality of Life principle recognizes that life is a necessary condition for other values and, as such, it recognizes a strong presumption in favor of preserving human life. Biologic human life is not an absolute value, but without it none of the other good things are possible. To prevent a callous disregard of human life, as reflected in the letters of I. G. Farben, this presumption must be emphasized and locutions such as "the sanctity of life," properly understood, may play a valuable role.

If this is correct, then the idea that life is sacred or valuable is, at best, of symbolic value, a shorthand for saying that the good things in life (rational self-consciousness, happiness, knowledge, love, justice, and so forth) should be promoted. The notion by itself needs interpretation. By itself it doesn't inform us on any major moral problem. Even if we agree that rational or human life is more valuable than the life of an ant or a rat, this doesn't deal with the crucial issues of quality. It does tell us not to take innocent life, but it doesn't tell us whether abortion or voluntary euthanasia are sometimes justified. It doesn't tell us whether capital punishment is sometimes valid. Nor does it speak one way or the other on the issues of suicide, vegetarianism, or animal research. It doesn't even tell us whether we should abandon or curtail the use of automobiles and adopt other modes of transportation. In all of these cases quality of life considerations need to enter into our deliberations. This is what we will be doing in examining the life and death issues in the rest of this book.

Study Questions

1. Explain the Sanctity of Life principle. What are its strengths and weaknesses? What are the far-reaching implications of adhering to it?

2. Can you believe in the sanctity of life without believing in a religion? Can a secularist hold the Sanctity of Life view? Why or why not?

3. Discuss Albert Schweitzer's "Reverence for Life" principle.

4. Contrast the Sanctity of Life principle with the Quality of Life principle. What are the key differences?

5. Socrates said, "The unexamined life is not worth living," and Jesus said of his betrayer, "It were better that he were never born." Do these statements support the Quality of Life principle over the Sanctity of Life principle.

6. How do the three major ethical theories view the Quality of Life/ Sanctity of Life dispute?

Endnotes

1. Albert Schweitzer, *Civilization and Ethics* (Part II of *The Philosophy of Civilization*), John Naish, trans. (London: Macmillan Publishing Co., 1929), p. 246.

2. Norman Cantor, "A Patient's Decision to Decline Lifesaving Medical Treatment: Bodily Integrity Versus the Preservation of Life," *Rutgers Law Review* 26 (Winter 1973), pp. 228–264.

3. Schweitzer, op. cit., pp. 246–247.

4. Byron Sherwin, "Jewish Views of Euthanasia," in Marvin Kohl's *Beneficent Euthanasia* (Buffalo: Prometheus, 1975), p. 7.

5. Paul Ramsey, "The Morality of Abortion," in James Rachels, ed., *Moral Problems* (New York: Harper & Row, 1971), pp. 11–13.

6. Moshe Tendler, quoted in Edward Keyserlingk's *Sanctity of Life or Quality of Life* (Law Reform Commission of Canada, 1982), p. 21. Tendler's logic might prevent us from brushing our teeth or washing, for if each part of a human is holy, each cell should be kept alive.

7. Anthony Shaw, "Dilemmas of 'Informed Consent' in Children," *New England Journal of Medicine* 289 17 (1973).

8. Paul Ramsey, *Ethics at the Edges of Life* (New Haven: Yale University Press, 1978), p. 191.

9. *The Federal Register* 49 (238), 48160.

10. Immanuel Kant, *Foundations of the Metaphysics of Morals*, Lewis Beck, trans. (Indianapolis: Bobbs-Merrill, 1959), p. 46.

11. Quoted in Bruno Bettleheim, *The Informed Heart* (London: Macmillan, 1960), ch. 6.

CHAPTER 3

Death and Dying

Normally we admire and praise the person who reaches his or her goal sooner than others. The first runner to reach the finish line, the climber to reach a mountain peak in the shortest time, the first person to fly the Atlantic Ocean, the first baseball pitcher to win 400 games, the first person to figure out a difficult problem, the youngest person to graduate from college or medical school; these people accomplish worthy feats that challenge us and draw our praise. Generally, the quicker we reach our goal or end, the better. The one exception is death. Although it is the end of life, that which every human and animal is destined to end up at, rare is the person in a hurry to die. All of us will die sooner or later. We are all traveling on different roads to the same destination. All roads lead, not to Rome, but to the grave.

We are all moving nearer to our end. This minute you are closer to death than the last minute, today you are closer to death than yesterday, this year closer than last year, and tomorrow you will be closer to it than today. People impatient for the future puzzle me because they are moving closer to their end. As St. Augustine said, "Any space of time that we live through leaves us with so much less time to live, and the remainder decreases with every passing day; so that the whole of our lifetime is nothing but a race towards death, in which no one is allowed the slightest pause or any slackening of the pace."[1]

I, like many of you, have experienced the psychologic equivalent of an earthquake at the death of my loved ones and heros. I remember the deep tremors of death's dance when my parents and two brothers died. I along with many people throughout America and the world glimpsed death's grim visage one November afternoon in 1963 when President John F. Kennedy was assassinated, and then when Martin Luther King Jr. was murdered in April 1968. But the death that shook the foundations of my soul was that of my teenage friend, George, the star of our high school football team. It occurred in the early summer after our sophomore year in high school. George, having been told by his physician that he had a heart murmur that would prevent him from ever again playing football, went up into his attic and hanged himself. The whole town of Cicero, Illinois, was shaken by this repudiation of existence, but no one more than me. For 2 weeks I walked in a daze, dizzy, disoriented, dumb with pain. My world had collapsed, my happy childhood abruptly ended. I wished that I were dead with George.

Gradually, I recovered and became deeply religious as a result of this tragedy, but the sense of loss has followed me throughout life. You don't fully recover from these catastrophes, though they tend to lend life perspective.

Death comes to everyone. It's a dark kingdom from which no visitors return, as Hamlet put it, a solemn mystery that from time immemorial has moved men and women to deep fear. It has inspired people to set up monuments in their memory, beget children as tokens of their immortality, fight holy wars, renounce the normal pleasures of life, leave their families and give themselves entirely to religion. Pyramids and cathedrals have been erected on the fear of death and hope of immortality.

What should be our attitude toward death?

The Western tradition has had five classic views of death: the Old Testament–Hebrew view, the Platonic–Christian view, the Epicurean view, the Stoic view, and the Existential view. Each one proposes a different response to this uninvited guest. We will better understand the meaning of death and dying if we examine each of these. You the reader may be able to combine some of these into a stronger position, or you may have to contribute a sixth position.

VIEWS OF DEATH IN WESTERN SOCIETY

The Old Testament–Hebrew View: Death as Punishment

There is no clear notion of immortality in the Hebrew Bible. Death is seen as punishment for sin—namely, the sin of our first parents, Adam and Eve, who were thrown out of the Garden of Eden because of disobedience. As children of fallen parents, all humans must taste death. "For dust thou art, and unto dust shalt thou return" (Gen 3:19). What is ultimately important for the Hebrews is not the individual but the nation Israel. A person has identity through the nation and through one's progeny or family within that nation, so that you will continue to live in the *memory* of the tribe long after you are gone—unless you have been immoral, in which case "may your memory be blotted from the earth." The fate worse than death is to be forgotten by the group.

The lack of a notion of an afterlife in Hebrew thought is paralleled by the ancient Greeks, as reflected by Homer, who said that he would rather be a servant on earth than reign in Hades, the land of the dead, where souls dwelt in a shadowy, passive, sleeplike existence.

It should be added that much of Judaism, especially the Pharisaic Judaism, by the time of Christ had accepted the doctrine of eternal life as do Orthodox Jews today.

The Platonic-Christian View: Immortality and Resurrection

The Greek philosopher Plato (427–347 B.C.) and Christian doctrine share a common fundamental idea with Orthodox Judaism, Islam, and Hinduism: Death is not the end of conscious life. Death, as the end of conscious existence, is an illusion. We survive our "deaths" in another world or in another form.

Look at the the Platonic view. Some of us were taught the following prayer:

> Now I lay me down to sleep,
> I pray the Lord my soul to keep,
> If I should die before I wake,
> I pray the Lord my soul to take.

This prayer is often taught in Sunday School or by parents who thought that it was the Christian view of the matter. But actually, the notion of the soul departing from the body is not Christian in origin. It's a Greek notion, and the prayer expresses a non-Christian view of death and eternal life.

Among the ancient Greeks, Pythagoras (fifth century B.C.) and Plato believed that the soul was immortal, having neither beginning nor end. In a previous immortal existence we learned the essential truths about the True, the Good, and the Beautiful. Thus, we have the capacity for knowledge, moral action, and the appreciation of beauty, regardless of how we've been brought up. Depending on how we live this life, we will be reincarnated in a future earthly existence into a bodily form fitting our moral worth in this life. People who live like pigs will become such, people who live nobly will be born with added talents and opportunities. At the end of the pilgrimage of existence the soul is merged with the GOOD, the essence of God.

For Plato the rational soul was lodged within the body as a tomb and at death was liberated from this clay coffin. Philosophy, for the Greeks, was a process of learning to die, learning to liberate oneself from the sensual, material nature of existence by purifying the soul through rational living. For the philosopher death becomes welcome relief, a rite of passage to a higher existence.

In the Christian view of death, Christ promised eternal life after death in a spiritual world in the presence of God. The support for this claim is Christ's resurrection from the dead, which is viewed as the model of our resurrection to eternal life. For the Christian, death, as the end of conscious life, really doesn't exist. As Paul says: "O death, where is thy sting? O grave where is thy victory? The sting of death is sin; and the strength of sin is the law. But thanks be to God, which giveth us the victory through our Lord Jesus Christ." (I Cor 15:55–57).

Although Christianty does not have a concept of a separate soul that is immortal, the *person* is created with eternity within him or her. We cannot die but will inhabit a godless hell or a God-filled heaven after death. For the believer death really doesn't exist. Eternal blessedness awaits the faithful, though it is not a soul but a transformed glorified body that inherits heaven.

The view is aptly illustrated by Benjamin Franklin, who had the following inscription prepared for his tombstone, which you may see in Philadelphia.

> The Body of Benjamin Franklin in Christ Church cemetery,
> Printer, Like the Cover of an Old Book,
> Its contents torn out,
> And stript of its Lettering and Guilding,
> Lies here, Food for Worms.
> But the work shall not be lost;
> For it will, as he believed,
> Appear once more in a new and more elegant Edition.
> Corrected and Improved by its Author.

This reconstituted self in a glorified body where the essential identity of the person is preserved is the hallmark of the Christian perspective on survival of death.

One of the most moving episodes of life is to witness the death of a believer. When the devout Oxford University scientist Charles Coulson, who was terminally ill with cancer, knew he had only a few weeks to live, he made appointments to see all his friends. They came to see him, one by one, spoke of the meaning of their friendship and their lives, and left deeply moved by the wisdom and humor of this saintly man who could stare death in the face and fearlessly smile. As the last guest left the room, Coulson expired in deep peace. His funeral was marked by so much joy and celebration over his life that passersby thought a wedding was taking place.

Of the early Christians martyrs, who were often devoured by lions or burnt at the stake, and who died singing praises to God and forgiving their executioners, it was said that their nobility in dying was evidence of the truth of their beliefs. "Behold how they die!" was a common comment on their brave martyrdom in the Roman world, as their blood became the seed of the Church.

The Epicurean View of Death: Secular Mortality

Epicurus (341–270 B.C.) believed that it is irrational to fear death. If there were an afterlife with punishments, you might be justified in having fear; but since there is absolutely no reason to believe that there is an afterlife (especially since we are material beings without souls), it is irrational to worry about future existence.

> Death is nothing to us. It does not concern either the living or the dead; since for the former it is not, and the latter are no more.
>
> Death is not to be feared, for Death and I never meet and no one should fear what he will never meet. We shall never meet, for when and where I am, Death is not; and where and when Death is, I am not. Hence there is nothing to fear from Death.

What we never meet, we have no reason to fear. So it's irrational to fear death. In essence the Epicureans deny death.

Leonardo da Vinci held that just as a day well spent brings happy sleep, so a life well spent should bring a happy death. A happy person is not seriously pained by the thought of death, nor does he or she morbidly dwell on the subject.

The motto, "Eat, drink, and be merry, for tomorrow we die," originates with the Epicureans. Put the thought of death out of your mind and enjoy life while it lasts. Contrary to common belief, the Epicurean life was actually quite moderate, not a gourmet or gluttonous, hedonistic life (in the contemporary sense). Epicurus advocated a tranquil, communal existence, "Far from the madding crowd," where cultured friends indulged not in sexual orgies but in refined conversation, literary excursions, and artistic delights—all accompanied by modest amounts of wine and cheese.

The Stoic View of Death: Creative Resignation

Zeno (335–264 B.C.), the founder of Stoicism, Cicero (106–43 B.C.), and Epictetus (A.D. 60–138) believed that while we could not control our external destiny, we could completely control our internal attitude toward our destiny. They taught that rational persons ought to resign themselves to their destiny and accept the inevitable. "If you can't get what you desire, desire what you get!"

We can overcome the fear of death by thinking about it constantly and in the proper manner. Life is a banquet from which we ought to retire at the proper time graciously and gratefully—possibly through suicide. Here is how the Stoic philosopher Seneca (A.D.3 – 65) put it:[2]

> Life has carried some men with the greatest rapidity to the harbor, the harbor they were bound to reach if they tarried on the way, while others it has fretted and harassed. To such a life, as you are aware, one should not always cling. *For mere living is not a good, but living well.* Accordingly, the wise man will live as long as he ought, not as long as he can. He will mark in what place, with whom, and how he is to conduct his existence, and what he is about to do. He always reflects concerning the quality, and not the quantity of his life. As soon as there are many events in his life that give him trouble and disturb his peace of mind, he sets himself free. And this privilege is his, not only when the crisis is upon him, but as soon as Fortune seems to be playing him false; then he looks about carefully and sees whether he ought, or ought not, to end his life on that account . . . He does not regard death with fear, as if it were a great loss; for no man can lose very much when but a driblet remains. It is not a question of dying earlier or later, but of dying well or ill. And dying well means escape from the danger of living ill.

Similarly, Shakespeare's Julius Caesar exemplifies Stoic resignation,[3]

> Cowards die many times before their death,
> The valiant never taste death but once.
> Of all the wonders that I yet have heard,
> It seems to me most strange that men should fear,
> Seeing that death, a necessary end,
> Will come when it will come.

The German philosopher Martin Heidegger echoed a Stoic theme when he said that death is our last act, which gives point to life. Dying is the one thing no one can do for you; you must die alone. To shut out the consciousness of death is therefore to refuse your own freedom and individuality; it is to refuse to live authentically. Death is the last chord in the symphony of our lives, which reverberates through all that has gone before, giving it meaning.

While Stoicism was marked by resignation, it was not a passive resignation, but an active one, committed to making the best of a person's lot. It was a philosophy that emphasized doing one's daily duty as though today were the last day of one's life. That is, the thought of death concentrated one's mind to squeeze all the nectar out of the living fruit of our finite existence. As a second-century Stoic, the Roman

Emperor Marcus Aurelius said, "Hour by hour resolve to do the task of the hour carefully, with unaffected dignity, affectionately, freely and justly. You can avoid distractions that might interfere with such performance if every act is done as though it were the last act of your life. Free yourself from random aims and curb any tendency to let the passions of emotion, hypocrisy, self-love and dissatisfaction with your allotted share cause you to ignore the commands of reason."[4]

The modern equivalent to Marcus Aurelius's credo is a well-known prayer by Reinhold Niebuhr.

> Lord, Give me the courage to change the things which can be changed. And give me the patience to accept the things that cannot be changed. But most of all, give me the wisdom to know the difference.

Wisdom lies in living a life that knows when to exercise courage and when to exercise resignation. Death is a case where both are called for. We resign ourselves to the unalterable fact that we will die, but we courageously overcome any useless perturbations over that fact.

Creative resignation learns to live gracefully with the tragedy of death; it lets the thought of death concentrate the mind so that we may more intensely appreciate each moment of life.

The Existential View of Death: Death as Absurd

Existentialists hold that death is meaningless and absurd, and that it shows that life is utterly meaningless and absurd. Schopenhauer believed this and advocated grim recognition and resignation. Life—what is left of it—should go on in aesthetic contemplation. Nietzsche taught that the Superman will be constantly aware of death in all its power and will not permit death to seek him out in ambush, to strike him down unawares. The Superman will be constantly aware of death, joyfully and proudly accepting death as the natural end of life. In this, the existentialists are similar to the stoics.

Albert Camus in his essay *The Myth of Sisyphus* asserted that the only interesting philosophic question is, "Why not commit suicide?" Since life is absurd, utterly meaningless, we are hard put to find a reason to continue living. His solution to the problem of absurdity is to rebel, to live defiantly in the midst of absudity.

Jean-Paul Sartre sees death as an absurdity, proving that life is absurd, that we are *de trop* (superfluous, unnecessary). Humans strive for permanency, to be God or eternal, but death puts an end to such grandiose projects and proves them ridiculous. There is just Nothingness, endless Nothingness, and we are Nothings. In the light of Nihilism, it doesn't matter what we do; yet we're absolutely free, "condemned to freedom," condemned to create our own absurd life projects in spite of their fundamental meaninglessness.

Where is the truth in these matters? The Existentialist view is the most pessimistic. Although some existentialists affirm that the creative use of our freedom produces personal value, this contradicts their idea that there are no objective values, that it really doesn't matter how we live. But Existentialism may give up too easily, for even if there is no afterlife, it doesn't mean that this life cannot be good in its own right. Life need not be absurd. Finite happiness is still happiness, a worthy existence. The Epicurean view is too unreflective, a naive case of self-deception. It's simply sophistry! Perhaps we don't "die" in the Epicurean sense of meeting death, but our consciousness comes to an end, we leave our friends and loved ones forever. And that is sad.

The Platonic–Christian view is the most optimistic. It has a certain logic in its favor, for it has the only chance of being *verified*, while it can't be *disproven*. For if life continues after death, then both the disbeliever and the believer will experience it, but if no life occurs after death, then the disbeliever will never be able to prove it to himself or herself or to the believer—because they will both be annihilated.

However, the Platonic-Christian View suffers the handicap of not having much strong evidence in its favor. The doctrine of reincarnation seems flawed because of good evidence that personality is a function of brain states, not some separate soul that transmigrates. In fact the notion of a simple soul unconnected to sense organs and the brain's memories seems like an empty concept. Furthermore, it's hard to see why reincarnation should comfort us. If my soul was once Abraham Lincoln's soul, but I am not Abraham Lincoln, then having inherited someone else's soul is about as comforting as inheriting someone else's genes. My children have inherited half of my genes, but they are not me. Likewise, even if some future person will inherit my soul, that won't be me—but a sort of descendant.

With regard to immortality in general, the problem for many of us who would like to believe in life after death is simply that people don't come back from the dead and describe its geography or climate.

In my philosophy classes I often ask the students, "How many here believe that there is life after death?" Usually 99 percent raise their hands—especially at the University of Notre Dame and the University of Mississippi, where I've taught. Then I ask them, "How many of you (as good Jews or Christians) believe that you are going to Heaven when you die?" About the same number of hands go up.

Then I ask, "How many of you believe that Heaven is infinitely more blissful than this corrupt earthly existence?" All hands go up.

"How many of you want to go to this wonderful place, right now?" I ask. Usually no one raises his or her hand. Such is the gap between religious profession and actual belief.

Nevertheless, perhaps there is some indirect evidence for survival after death. James Moody documents several cases of clinically dead persons, who on being revived reported remarkably similar out-of-the-body (or *near-death*) experiences. Moody sets down an idealized report in the following passage:[5]

> A man is dying and, as he reaches the point of greatest distress, he hears himself pronounced dead by his doctor. He begins to hear an uncomfortable noise, a loud ringing or buzzing, and at the same time feels himself moving outside of his own physical body from a distance, as though he is a spectator. He watches the resuscitation attempt from this unusual vantage point as in a state of emotional upheaval.
>
> After a while, he collects himself and becomes more accustomed to his odd condition. He notices that he still has a "body," but one of a very different nature and with very different powers from the physical body he has left behind. Soon other things begin to happen. Others come to meet and to help him. He glimpses the spirits of relatives and friends who have already died, and a loving, warm spirit of a kind he has never encountered before—a being of light—appears before him. This being asks him a question, nonverbally, to make him evaluate his life and helps him along by showing him a panoramic, instantaneous playback of the major events of his life. At some point he finds himself approaching some sort of barrier or border, apparently representing the limit between earthly life and the next life. Yet, he finds that he must go back to the earth, that the time for his death has not yet come. At this point he resists, for by now he is taken up with his experiences in the afterlife and does not want to return. He is overwhelmed by intense feelings of joy, love, and peace. Despite his attitude, though, he somehow reunites with his physical body and lives.

This passage is not meant to represent any one person's report but is a composite of the common elements found in many stories. Moody himself makes no claims for the interpretation that the patients really experienced what they claimed to have experienced. Neurologic causes might account for these experiences, or they could be attributed to wish fulfillment. But these experiences should be included with all our other thinking on this matter and should be followed up with further research. The reports may allow some of us to live in a rationally based hope of immortality.

Is the fear of death universal? Freud, Ernest Becker, and other psychoanalysts thought so, but I doubt it. It seems to occur primarily where heightened self-consciousness arises, where individualism takes root, and individuals values their own existence more than the group's. Primitive human beings, like animals or Adam and Eve in the paradisiacal garden, are unemcumbered by perturbations of mortality. Small children do not seem to fear death, and it is likely that primitive humans who identified with the tribe probably didn't fear death the way the modern European or American does. Aldous Huxley, in his classic, prophetic novel, *Brave New World,* describes people bred on *soma* and sensuous feelies who lack deep self-consciousness and hence the fear of death. You may differ with me here, but then you should work out an alternate account of the fear of death.

Death seems a natural event, not something that has been imposed on us from without as punishment for sin, but it is still perceived as an evil once we understand what it implies. We come to fear it as our sense of self develops. Children between the ages of three and six frequently express horror at the idea of their own future demise. On hearing that a relative died, my 3-year old daughter asked me, "Will I die too, Daddy?"

"Yes," I answered.

"But I don't want to. I won't do it!"

Tears filled her eyes and replaced her defiant words as it dawned on her that death wasn't something over which she had any control. It happens whether we like it or not.

Death is an evil. As persons we have desires and projects. When these desires and projects are satisfied, we are usually happy. When they are not, we are frustrated. To the extent that our values are not realized in the world, to that extent the world is evil for us. But in death all our desires are finally frustrated, all our projects taken away from us. All that we value is separated from us forever. We are removed permanently from all we value: our loved ones, conscious experience, our work, beauty, creativity, pleasure, happiness, and knowledge. We will never again hear the song of birds, smell the fragrance of flowers, or hear the laughing voices of children. Hence death must be seen both as natural and as evil.

Nevertheless, though death is an evil, and fear has to do with being confronted by the prospect of such evil, we ought not fear death. Epicurus was the first philosopher to argue that we ought not fear death, since we should not fear things that we will never encounter and death and I will never meet. "For when it is, I am not, and when I am, it is not." Although this argument states our relationship to death in a misleading fashion, there is some truth in its message that it is irrational to fear death. Let me explain.

What distinguishes rational from irrational fear? Rational fear has to do with avoiding what is harmful and can be avoided. The fear of fire causes us to keep our distance from it. The fear of danger causes us to stay out of some neighborhoods at night. The fear of cancer causes some people to stop smoking. The fear of AIDS causes people to restrain their sexual proclivities. Rational fear is purposive and instrumental to reaching worthy goals such as good health.

But irrational fear is not instrumental in this way. A fear of water (hydrophobia) keeps you from enjoying some good things, like swimming and boating. A fear of people, sex, or love is disastrous to our personal growth. Some people suffer irrational anxiety for no apparent reason or go through life as guilt gluttons, feeling remorse for what they could in no way have prevented. This is the truth of Epicurus's dictum that we ought not to fear death since the two of us will never meet. It is not that we never meet, but that the meeting is unavoidable and what is unavoidable ought to be met with resignation and courage, as the Stoics counsel us.

Deeply engrained within our psyche as it is, thanophobia (fear of death) can be conquered, if not altogether, then to a great extent. We can learn to smile at the Grim Reaper. We may have to go through a mental practice, such as yoga, Stoic resignation, prayer, or meditation on the nature of things, but we can become wise regarding this inevitable event. Of course, we will still have an aversion to death and try to prolong life with happiness as long as possible, and we will still fear an agonizing or demeaning death with loss of dignity. But death itself is not to be feared; that fear can be conquered through reason and the will. We can live like a Stoic, letting the thought of death concentrate the mind to get the most out of life.

In the ancient Greek myth, Sisyphus is condemned by the gods to rolling a huge stone up the side of a mountain until it reaches the top, whereupon the stone rolls down to the bottom and Sisyphus must follow its course and retrieve it. He goes through the process again and again for all eternity. Tedious, boring, meaningless, such is the process of this neverending toil. But Sisyphus, if he is sufficiently resourceful, can find meaning in his toil. As Camus recognizes, " The struggle towards the heights [in life] is enough to fill a person's heart. One must imagine Sisyphus happy."[6]

And so it is with us. We can find meaning to life in the midst of our labors, even though we, unlike Sisyphus, will die. The wise person will accept the inevitability of all good things coming to an end, including life, and treating life as a glorious banquet: having been enjoyed to the full but now coming to a close, he or she retires gracefully, grateful for all the good things experienced. Death becomes a way of saying thank you.

Study Questions

1. What are the five classic views of death in Western society? Which one, if any, do you believe in and why?

2. Discuss James Moody's description of out-of-body experiences. Does the evidence available support the view that there is life after death?

3. Is death an evil? Is the fear of death rational? If it is irrational, can such fear be overcome? Explain.

4. How does the fact that you will die affect your value system? The way you live? Does the fact of death help us understand the meaning of life?

5. If there is no God and no life after death, does it make any difference how we live? Is life absurd?

Endnotes

1. St. Augustine, *City of God*, ch. 13.
2. Seneca, "On Suicide," in *Epistula Morales*, vol. II. R. M. Gumere, trans. (Cambridge: Harvard University Press, 1920), p. 54.
3. William Shakespeare, *Julius Caesar*, Act II, Scene II.
4. Marcus Aurelius, *Meditations*, Book Ten.
5. James Moody, *Life after Life* (New York: Bantam Books, 1976), pp. 21f.
6. Albert Camus, *The Myth of Sisyphus*, Justin O'Brien, trans. (New York: Vintage Books, 1960), p. 91.

CHAPTER 4

Suicide

A few years ago I was on a fellowship at a major medical center. The following situation arose on the intensive care unit and was discussed at a case conference. A Korean woman, Mrs. C, who was on a ventilator and being fed through a nasogastric tube, asked to have the ventilator removed so that she could die. Mrs. C had married an American soldier in Korea against the wishes of her parents and, hence, had been disowned by them. She came to America, got a divorce, remarried, and had a son. But guilt and shame haunted her throughout her life. She felt a total failure and was often deeply depressed. She attempted suicide eight times, failing each time. On her eighth attempt, she put a gun to her head and pulled the trigger. The pistol jolted, and instead of going through her head, the bullet went through her neck, paralyzing her from the neck down. She was a quadriplegic. Now she wanted to be left to die.

Mrs. C's husband and 10-year-old son were called in. Both loved her and wanted her to live, but they also respected her wishes and were willing to let go and allow her to die, if that was her wish.

The physicians, psychiatrists, therapists, nurses, and hospital administrators argued the case out. About half of those involved believed that the woman should be allowed to die, the other half holding that she should be kept alive and given extensive psychologic counseling. What was the right thing to do? How are the patient's wishes in such cases to be balanced by the principle of preserving conscious life? Doctors have been trained to save life, above all "to do no harm." Are we now calling on them to change their basic philosophy of medicine?

Mrs. C's case forces us to reconsider our views on suicide, as well as euthanasia. When if ever does a person have a right to take his or her own life? Is suicide ever morally permissible? Since the most controversial kinds of euthanasia are extensions of the notion of suicide, let us first get clear on the ethical status of suicide before we turn to the problem of euthanasia.

Suicide is a taboo subject in our society. Whereas our ancestors spoke openly of death, including suicide, and were silent on sex, we are garrulous on sex, but silent on death, especially suicide. Bring it up at the next party to which you're invited and you won't have to worry about party clothes for a long time.

Earlier I spoke of the experience of losing a loved one as the psychologic equivalent of an earthquake. The earthquake in the case of suicide registers around 10 on the Richter Scale—its force is compounded by the horror of its cosmic irreverence. Suicide shakes the foundations of the entire structure of our values. In one fell swoop all that we take for granted in daily life has been put in question. Here is someone who has refused to "suffer the slings and arrows of outrageous fortune" and has taken arms against them, as Hamlet once contemplated.

Can one ever make a rational decision to kill oneself? Is it ever moral to commit suicide?

Suicide can be defined as an act in which a person intentionally brings about his or her own death in circumstances where others do not coerce that person to act. That is, (1) death is intended by the agent, (2) it is caused by the agent, and (3) no one else is forcing the agent to this killing of self. We also distinguish between (a) self-regarding and (b) altruistic suicides, the former being done to eliminate suffering of the self while the latter eliminates suffering or even the death of others.

The first condition, intentionality, rules out "slow-motion suicides," such as that discussed by the sociologist Ronald Maris[1]: "Suicide occurs when an individual engages in a lifestyle that he knows might kill him ...and it does [kill him]. This is an omnibus definition of suicide, which includes various forms of self-destruction, such as risk-taking and many so-called 'accidents.'" Ian Martin identifies overdrinking and smoking with attempted suicide.[2] But by this omnibus definition we could get the strange situation of a woman who is murdered while walking through a dangerous neighborhood in order to get home. The murderer pleads, "Ms. Jones committed suicide knowing, as she did, the danger of our neighborhood. I can't be tried for murder—only for assisting in a suicide." The omnibus definition is too "omni-"; it takes purpose out of the act.

There is a question about whether the agent must have strictly intended his or her death or simply voluntarily caused it. Consider the following news release.

The American soldier who threw himself on an exploding grenade to save his comrades during a fierce fight in Viet Nam was identified as Daniel Fernandez of Los Lunas, N.M. Under intense enemy pressure the unit fell back carrying their wounded with them, but the Viet Cong followed up with rifle and grenade fire. Fernandez was reported to have jumped on a Viet Cong grenade and covered it with his body to shield other members of his unit from the explosive blast which killed him. "He sacrificed himself to save us," one of his buddies said. (Associated Press Report, February 1966)

Fernandez seems to have voluntarily caused his own death, but did he commit suicide? If you think that *voluntarily and knowingly* causing one's own death is sufficient to constitute a suicide, you will say that Fernandez committed suicide. If you take *intended* more strictly, you will say that he did not commit suicide, for he didn't jump on the enemy grenade in order to die but to save his fellows.

A borderline case is that of the sickly Captain Oates who walked out of Scott's tent on the Antarctic expedition to save the expeditionary party. Did Oates commit suicide? Ethicists have debated this back and forth. Roy Holland argues that he did not commit suicide because he merely intended to relieve his party of his presence. " The blizzard killed him. Had Oates taken out a revolver and shot himself I should have agreed he was a suicide."[3] In such cases as these, there seems to be a fine line between knowing the certain consequences of your actions and intending that those consequences take place.

In one sense, it doesn't matter what we call these cases as long as we agree on the moral status of the acts. We can say that they were suicides, but morally good—altruistic—acts, so that it turns out that some suicides are justified or permitted. Or we can say that Fernandez and Oates's acts were not suicides but acts of voluntarily causing their own death. I'm inclined to say that Fernandez's act was not a suicide. In the spontaneity of the moment, his thought may only have been to protect his comrades. The distinct intention of dying was lacking. The fact that Oates premeditated on his act and voluntarily took steps to ensure his death puts his act closer to what we would call a suicide.

But what about the Buddhist monk who immolates himself to protest a tyrannical government? Or Sidney Carton in Dickens's *Tale of Two Cities* who takes the place of his friend and goes to the guillotine? Here an intention to die is present, so that we should agree that the monk and Carton both committed suicide.

Interestingly, the early Christian theologians Tertullian (150–220) and Origin (182–254) believed that Jesus committed suicide, intending to die for the world's salvation by voluntarily giving up the ghost. If they are correct, the crucifixion was an altruistic suicide.

The suicide need not be an overt act. As long as the intention is present, allowing oneself to die is sufficient. Sidney Carton voluntarily walked to the guillotine, but he did not pull the blade down on his neck. If I wish to die and hire you to pull the plug on my ventilator, in a sense I've committed suicide and you've committed allocide (assisting in a suicide). Likewise, if someone accidentally cuts with a knife so that I bleed, and I deliberately do not stanch the flow of blood, I have (passively) committed self-slaughter.

Whether they are called "suicide" or "voluntary self-slaughter," society has always praised altruistic or other-regarding suicides. But self-regarding suicide has suffered just the opposite judgment. It is the paradigm of cowardly or selfish action, of taking fate into one's own hands, a sin against God. Wittgenstein expresses a widespread sense of horror at such self-demise. "If suicide is allowed then everything is allowed. If anything is not allowed then suicide is not allowed. This throws a light on the nature of ethics, for suicide is, so to speak, the elementary sin."[4]

Yet until the sixth century Christianity not only tolerated suicide but praised a form of martyrdom that bordered on suicide. There is no word against suicide in the Old Testament, where four suicides are recorded without adverse comment, or in the New Testament, where Judas Iscariot hangs himself. At Masada (A.D. 72) Eleazar led some 900 Jews in a mass suicide rather than be captured by the Romans. As I mentioned earlier, the leading Christian theologians Tertullian and Origin regarded Jesus' death as a suicide, noting that he voluntarily "gave up the ghost." Early Christians often embraced martyrdom willingly, sometimes paying strangers to kill them so they might enter Heaven immediately. Virgins killed themselves to prevent being raped. "Let me enjoy those beasts," exclaimed the Christian martyr Ignatius in the second century, "whom I wish more cruel than they are; for if they will not attack me, I will provoke and draw them by force." Gibbon tells us that one Christian sect, the Donatists, "frequently stopped travellers on the public highways and obliged them to inflict the stroke of martyrdom by promise of a reward, if they consented—and by the threat of instant death, if they refused to grant so very singular a favor."[5]

It was Augustine, Bishop of Hippo (354–430), who in response to the growing loss of Christians in his domain through voluntary martyrdom first proclaimed that it was sinful, a violation of the Sixth Commandment, "Thou shalt not kill." Suicide was first condemned by the Church at the Council of Braga in 562, at which time people who committed suicide were denied funeral rites. In the next century attempted suicides were excommunicated from the Church, and later referred to as "martyrs for Satan." Thomas Aquinas (1225–1274) set forth the position of the Catholic Church, arguing that it was a mortal sin against God because it was against nature and charity, an offense against society, and a destruction of God's gift.

Since the sixth century suicide has been generally condemned in Western society and Aquinas's arguments have won widespread acceptance. Traditionally, Jews and Christians have condemned self-regarding suicide as an affront to God, because only God can give and take innocent life. Our lives are gifts of God. They are not owned by us but are God's property. We are stewards of His property. As Kant put it, "Human beings are sentinels on earth and may not leave their posts until relieved by another beneficent hand."[6]

This argument, which has been effective throughout Western history, has two drawbacks. First, if someone doesn't believe in God (or a God who keeps our lives as His property), the argument fails. Second, God is made into a monster, who forces us to endure torture and suffering. If the property–steward view of life were to hold, one would suppose God to take better care of His or Her possessions and to ameliorate the agony of existence more than God does. What kind of sentinel is the terminally ill cancer patient, lying in anguish with only 2 days to live? God has given us reason to use medicines to alleviate suffering in ourselves and others, and that could include the option of ending our existence when it becomes a burden to ourselves or our loved ones.

The second main argument against suicide is the argument from nature: It is natural to want to live and to promote life. This argument is simply confused. Nature both brings to life and kills. To kill and avoid pain and suffering are natural tendencies. What is unnatural about suicide? As David Hume says, "It would be no crime in me to divert the Nile or Danube from its course, were I able to effect such purposes. Where then is the crime of turning a few ounces of blood from their natural channel?"[7]

To want to live as long as life is pleasurable seems natural. Life itself, I have argued in Chapter 2, is not an absolute value.

If the property argument or the argument from nature were taken seriously, it would mean that we could not morally sacrifice our lives for others—for is it not playing God by going against nature to intervene in the death of others? Daniel Fernandez would have been forbidden to fall on the bomb that would have killed his comrades and Sidney Carton would be forbidden to give his life for his friend. Altruistic suicides, accepted by the Catholic Church, as well as self-regarding suicides would be condemned as immoral.

Suicide and the Meaning of Life

Albert Camus in his gem, *The Myth of Sisyphus,* calls suicide the "one truly philosophical problem."[8] Why not commit suicide? he asks. Consider his grim picture of absurd existence, the kind that, according to Camus, all of us live in one way or another.

On Monday morning a man or woman gets up at 6:30, goes to the toilet, washes, dresses, and eats breakfast. Another hour is spent mindlessly commuting to a job whose work when looked at with a lucid eye is ultimately purposeless. If it weren't for the grim need to earn wages, no sane person would do this kind of thing. Then, return: a mindless commute to a mindless evening before a mindless entertainment box, and then to bed. The saga is repeated Tuesday, Wednesday, Thursday, and Friday for over 40 years until the person retires, too old to discover a better way of life. Saturdays he or she spends recovering from the exhaustion of the other 5 days and on Sunday he or she is bored at the home of relatives or else, if not very sensitive, he or she enjoys inconsequential gossip about the food, weather, or football game. Occasionally, the person gets drunk or soothes his or her raging hormones in an act of lust.

The person's goal is to make enough money to feed and educate his or her children so that they can grow up to repeat this silly game, making enough money to feed and educate their children in order that they can play it too, and so on.

Camus asks us to discover some enduring value in this person's life. One day the person may wake up and discover that there isn't any.

Outraged at this analysis, you might protest, "Life is made meaningful by ameliorating the suffering in society, of bringing about revolution or reform." Perhaps. John Stuart Mill once thought the same. In his *Autobiography*[9] Mill describes the crisis of meaning that took place in his twenty-second year of life. Following Jeremy Bentham, Mill's whole life had been dedicated to social reform, and as long as he could see the world improving, he felt satisfaction and even happiness. But a crisis arose in 1826. He was in a "dull state of nerves, such as everybody is occasionally liable to," when the following question occurred to him, "'Suppose that all your objects in life were realized; that all the changes in institutions and opinions which you are looking forward to, could be completely effected at this very instant: would this be a great joy and happiness to you?' An irrepressible self consciousness distinctly answered, 'No!' At this my heart sank within me: the whole foundation on which my life was constructed fell down. All my happiness was to have been founded in the continual pursuit of this end. The end had ceased to charm, and how could there ever again be any interest in the means? I seemed to have nothing left to live for." Mill went through a deep depression that lasted several months, during which he came close to suicide. Ask yourself the same question he did.

Note, in this regard, how much "good work" is simply the negating of social negativities.[10] Some of the highest paid and most prestigious professions involve little more than ameliorating evils rather than creating good. The physician is a parasite on disease, without which he or she would be extraneous. The doctor doesn't produce any positive value but merely helps negate illness. The lawyer spends his or her time prosecuting or defending people accused of evil transactions, or in executing a will the lawyer becomes a partial heir to an estate to which the lawyer has no fundamental relation, or, like a cistern, he or she transfers wealth in costly litigation from one party to another, becoming a leaky pipe, siphoning off large doses of the principal. In malpractice suits the attorney may receive between 30 and 40 percent of the award. If people were honest, would we need lawyers to write up wills? If people were moral, where would the criminal lawyer be? If people's word were bond, would we need legal contracts? If people lived decently and rationally, how much litigation would there be? Of course, we need lawyers in a society filled with avarice and distrust, but the point is, according to this negative analysis, most of the lawyers' functions and earnings are based on human weakness and misery. Without human negativities, the lawyer's lot would be a poor one. The attorney is a negator of negativities.

So much of life is merely negating the negative in order to keep the status quo. It's as though we were in the middle of the ocean on a boat with numerous leaks in which our primary task was to bail out water so that we could simply stay afloat and sail in circles. Would we think a person who decided to call the whole game quits and jump into the ocean stupid or immoral? Certainly not stupid, for the game wasn't worth the bucket.

So why don't we commit suicide?

The answer has to do with what is valuable, what makes life worth living. While life itself may be neither good nor bad, it is the necessary condition for whatever is good or bad. And there are good things in life: living in loving relationship with spouse, friends, and children; learning about the world—both the external world of physics, chemistry, biology, and so on and the internal world of self and other; creating works of art and music; writing a sonnet or planning a dinner; becoming an ideal person, a spiritual work of art; becoming accomplished at a complex skill or interesting activity; enjoying simple and profound pleasures. Alleviating suffering and pain also gives life meaning. Although these negatings of negatives are not sufficient to make life positively worthwhile, the hope in pursuing social justice is that by removing the injustice or suffering, the victim will find positive meaning. That makes negating the negations worthwhile.

What happens when these values are irretrievably lost? What happens when health, so important for the attainment of most of the other values, is going or is gone? When human relations are hopelessly destroyed? When our mind loses its acuity so that we not only cease to learn the new but forget the old? When the pain becomes too great to bear? What happens when we have committed a grave evil and cannot make restitution, or when we find evil uncontrollably manifests itself in destroying others?

When life has lost the values that give it value, when its sum total is in the red, why is it wrong to put a stop to the misery, if one so desires?

Under some conditions suicide appears morally permissible. We have seen that altruistic ones are, for they are supererogatory acts aiming to help others. But other instances of suicide may also be justified if life becomes unbearable and no hope for remission is in sight. As Epictetus put it, "If the room is smoky, if only moderately, I will stay; if there is too much smoke, I will go. Remember this, keep a firm hold on it, the door is always open."

The right to die seems a corollary of our right to life itself, for what is a right if it cannot be waived? A right that cannot be waived is not a right but a duty. But a good argument against all forms of rational suicide has yet to be given, so there is no reason to suppose that all rational suicide is wrong. The only question is, what are the conditions for rational or morally permissible suicide? I suggest the following:

1. The person has made a realistic assessment of the situation and judges suicide to be the best course of action for him or her.
2. A reasonable time has elapsed for review of the situation.
3. The harm likely to be done to others resulting from the suicide is not likely to outweigh the amount of evil avoided to the person himself or herself.

Let us apply this to some cases. Take the case of a man dying of cancer, who is unable to find relief for his pain, who has settled his accounts, and now only has the prospect of further suffering and huge medical bills. He has fulfilled all three conditions. He knows that there is no hope of remission, a reasonable time of reflection about his case has transpired, and no great harm is likely to be done to others; indeed, he will be sparing them huge medical expenses if he kills himself. Why isn't this man justified in committing suicide? He has every right to do so, according to my criteria.

On the other hand, take the following cases of teen suicide. My friend George, mentioned at the beginning of the previous chapter, committed suicide on being told that his heart murmur would prevent him from playing football again, and two 16-year-olds, call them Len and Lisa, who when prevented by their parents from living together asphyxiated themselves to death in a car in the garage of Len's parents.

The tragedy of these kinds of suicides is matched only by their foolishness. None of the conditions mentioned above have been fulfilled. The teenager is usually in no position to make a realistic assessment of his or her situation. If only George had had the patience to wait a few months, he would have found new goals in life to replace football. If only Len and Lisa could wait a year or two, they would have grown out of their love or found a way to get married. Teenage suicides still fill us with horror because we see these young people throwing away their lives before they are lived. They are rejecting the goods that we feel sure are worth the trouble. Moreover, regarding the third condition, they are causing incalculable suffering to family, friends, and community who have strong emotional investments in them.

Given these conditions, suicide prevention and intervention programs should certainly be instituted to restrain and restore temporarily people who precipitously attempt suicide. The truth is, we all become depressed and in that state may lose lucidity. The philosopher Richard Brandt sums it up nicely[11]:

> Depression, like any severe emotional experience, tends to primitivize one's intellectual process. It restricts the range of one's survey of the possibilities. One thing that a rational person would do is compare the world-course containing his suicide with his best alternative. But his best alternative is precisely a possibility he may overlook if, in a depressed mood, he thinks only of how badly off he is and cannot imagine any way of improving his situation.

Evidence shows that a large percentage of attempted suicides are done in moments of high stress or in order to communicate with others.[12] Intervention is justified in these cases and counseling should commence.

But when it comes to elderly people who are losing their faculties, or terminally ill patients, or when rational adults have lost all that makes life worthwhile for them, their autonomy should be respected. While we regret these deaths, we do not feel the same sense of tragedy as we do with teenage suicides, where full autonomy is missing.

Janet Adkins had every right, after counseling, to take her life when the wine was running dry and she could look forward only to semiconsciousness. And the same is correct about Mrs. C, the Korean woman mentioned at the beginning of this chapter.

When Dr. and Mrs. Henry Van Dusen, the former President of Union Theological Seminary and his wife, committed suicide together in their eighties, it was done as an act of worship culminating two lives lived in the service of God and humanity. They had lived life to the fullest and decided to depart before their failing powers reduced them to shadows of their former selves and a burden on their children. Perhaps they should have consulted with their children, perhaps their suicides were premature, but we can understand the Van Dusens's concern about their failing powers and their being a burden to themselves and their children.

When it becomes clear beyond reasonable doubt that the nullity of death will be preferable to the negative value of a suffering life, the rational thing to do is act with dispatch.

Gradually, our society is coming to accept a limited version of this argument for morally permissible suicide. While we rightly deplore teenage suicides as unjustified because none of the relevant conditions have been fulfilled, we sympathize with the terminally ill patient who has no prospect for a happy life. We judge the elderly and terminally ill less severely.

Note that Barney Clark, the 61-year-old retired dentist and the first human being to receive a permanent artificial heart, was given a key that he could use to turn off the compressor if he should wish at any time to cease living attached to the machine.

> "If the man suffers and feels it isn't worth it any more, he has a key that he can apply," said Dr. Willem Kolff, head of the University of Utah's Artificial Organs Division, inventor of the artificial kidney, and founder of the artificial heart program.
>
> "I think it is entirely legitimate that this man whose life has been extended should have the right to cut it off if he doesn't want it, if life ceases to be enjoyable," he added.
>
> "The operation won't be a success unless he is happy. That has always been our criteria—to restore happiness."[13]

This sounds close to the Stoic doctrine of leaving the smoky room. "If the room is smoky, if only moderately, I will stay; if there is too much smoke, I will go. Remember this, keep a firm hold on it, the door is always open" (Epictetus).

Study Questions

1. Is suicide always immoral or is it sometimes morally permissible? If it is sometimes morally permissible, under what circumstances?

2. Is self-destructive behavior such as heavy smoking, overdrinking of alcoholic beverages, or drug abuse a form of indirect suicide? Explain.

3. Some people believe that suicide is wrong because it violates natural law. It simply goes against our natural tendency to want to live. Do you agree? What, if any, is the relationship between something being unnatural and its being immoral? Go back and look at David Hume's comment on this. Is Hume correct in comparing the suicide's opening of his or her blood vessel with the opening of a dam?

4. Why does Camus call suicide the only truly philosophic problem? Is he correct?

5. Under what circumstances should we engage in suicide prevention and under what circumstances, if any, should we refrain from interfering?

Endnotes

1. Ronald Maris, "Sociology," in S. Perlin, ed., *A Handbook for the Study of Suicide* (Oxford: Oxford University Press, 1975), p. 100.

2. Ian Martin, "Slow Motion Suicide," *New Society* (October 1974).

3. Roy Holland, "Suicide," in J. Rachels, ed,. *Moral Problems* (New York: Harper and Row, 1973).

4. Ludwig Wittgenstein, *Notebooks 1914–1916*, G. H. von Wright and G. E. M. Anscombe, eds. (Oxford: Basil Blackwell, 1961), p. 91.

5. Edward Gibbon, *The Decline and Fall of the Roman Empire* (1776), vol. III, p. 401.

6. Immanuel Kant, *Lectures on Ethics*, Louis Infield, trans. (New York: Harper & Row, 1963), p. 154.

7. David Hume, "Of Suicide," *Essays: Moral, Political and Literary* (Oxford: Oxford University Press, 1963), pp. 585–596.

8. Albert Camus, *The Myth of Sisyphus* (New York: Vintage Books, 1960), p. 3.

9. John Stuart Mill, *Autobiography*, (Oxford: Oxford University Press, 1873), p. 94.

10. In the next two paragraphs I am reflecting the existentialist perspective; it is not necessarily my own, although I think there is truth in it.

11. Richard Brandt, "The Morality and Rationality of Suicide," in Seymour Perlin, ed., *A Handbook for the Study of Suicide* (Oxford: Oxford University Press, 1975).

12. David Greenberg, "Interference with a Suicide Attempt," *New York University Law Review* 49 (May–June 1974), pp. 227–269.

13. Quoted in James Rachels, *The End of Life* (Oxford: Oxford University Press, 1986) p. 79.

CHAPTER 5

Euthanasia

The intentional termination of the life of one human being by another—mercy killing—is contrary to that for which the medical profession stands and is contrary to the policy of the American Medical Association.
The cessation of the employment of extraordinary means to prolong the life of the body when there is irrefutable evidence that biological death is imminent is the decision of the patient and/or his immediate family. The advice and judgment of the physician should be freely available to the patient and/or his immediate family.

—AMERICAN MEDICAL ASSOCIATION
POLICY STATEMENT ON VOLUNTARY EUTHANASIA

On April 14, 1975 Karen Ann Quinlan, a 21-year-old woman, lapsed into a coma from which she never emerged. Thus began the most famous case in the history of American medical ethics. The combination of Valium, aspirin, and three gin and tonics at a party may have deprived her brain of oxygen, causing extensive brain damage and a state of persistent vegetation that was to last 10 years, while the family, the hospital, and the courts angrily fought over her body. The national media caught every breath and blow in the action.

After months of watching their adopted daughter's body curled up in a fetal position and maintained by life supports, Joseph and Julia Quinlan despaired of hope, and with the approval of their priest they asked the physicians at St. Clare's Hospital in Danville, New Jersey, to disconnect the ventilator. Dr. Robert Morse, attending physician, agreed and had the Quinlans sign a form absolving him of liability. A few days later Morse, perhaps fearing a malpractice suit, changed his mind and refused to disconnect the ventilator, telling the Quinlans that since Karen was 21, they needed a court order appointing Mr. Quinlan as

Karen's legal guardian before the ventilator could be switched off. Karen was not brain dead under New Jersey law. There was some electroencephalographic activity, though neurologists agreed that her comatose condition was irreversible. Meanwhile Medicare was paying the medical costs of $450 per day.

The Quinlan's lawyer, Paul Armstrong, first argued that since Karen was brain dead, she should be unhooked from life-support systems. But when Judge Muir pointed out that Karen had not met the criteria for brain death under New Jersey law, Armstrong amended his brief, arguing for a right to die based on three grounds: religious freedom, cruel and unusual punishment, and the right to privacy. The first ground claimed that Karen's wish to die was based on her religious beliefs. The second compared the physicans at the hospital to prison guards who were punishing prisoners. The third, the "right to privacy," appealed to the 1973 *Roe v. Wade* abortion decision of the Supreme Court, which spoke of an individual's right to make personal decisions. The New Jersey Attorney General opposed pulling the plug, arguing that to do so "would open the door to euthanasia." Morse's lawyer, Ralph Porzio, argued that to allow Karen to die would start a slippery slope leading to the killing of people who lived a poor quality of life. "And fresh in our minds are the Nazi atrocities. Fresh in our minds are the human experimentations. Fresh in our minds are the Nuremberg Codes."[1]

Judge Muir accepted Porzio's arguments and proclaimed that the family's anguish over their comatose daughter was clouding their judgment.

In Rome, a Vatican theologian, Gino Concetti, condemned the act of removing Karen from life support systems. "A right to death does not exist. Love for life, even a life reduced to a ruin, drives one to protect life with every possible care."[2]

The case was appealed, and on January 26, 1976, the New Jersey Supreme Court overruled Judge Muir. It set aside all criminal liability in removing Karen from a respirator. St. Clare's Hospital, fearing bad publicity in allowing Karen's death, stalled and even added a second machine to control Karen's body temperature. Finally, after several weeks of waiting, Karen was weened off the ventilator. St. Clare's asked that she be transferred to another institution. But that proved difficult to do. Twenty hospitals and nursing homes refused to accept Karen before the Morris View Nursing Home took her in on June 9, 1976, some five and a half months after the court's decision to allow her to die.

For 9 years Karen Ann Quinlan lay in a comatose state on a waterbed in Morris View Nursing Home, artificially fed via a feeding tube. Each day her father would rise at 4:30 for a 40-mile drive to the nursing home where he would talk to Karen, massage her back and even sing to her. His comatose daughter was still a person to him. On June 11, 1985, Karen died.

The New York Times recently reported that presently over 10,000 people in the nation are in the same type of condition that Karen had been in. The most notable of these is Nancy Cruzon. In June 1990 the United States Supreme Court decided that unless there is a prior, clear proof of intent, the matter of allowing patients in a persistent vegetative state to die should be left up to individual states.[3]

The term *euthanasia* comes from the Greek and means "good death." *Webster's Dictionary* defines it as "a quiet and easy death" or "the action of inducing a quiet and easy death." Euthanasia can refer to inducing death either *passively* or *actively* —that is, either by withdrawing treatment or actively putting to death. It can also be divided into two types of patient intentions, where the patient has given consent and where the patient is not able to do so, that is, *voluntarily* and *involuntarily* (or nonvoluntarily). If we take these categories and combine them, we end up with four distinct types of euthanasia:

	Voluntary	*Involuntary*
Passive	Refusal of treatment No extraordinary means or heroic treatment	Withdrawing of treatment primarily on defective neonates, incompetent patients, and those in a persistent vegetative state
Active	Induce death with consent Allocide or mercy killing of hopeless cases with pain	Induce without consent Mercy killing Incompetent; deformed neonates

Active euthanasia is illegal throughout the United States, though under considerable debate. Passive euthanasia has long been practiced. Its application under modern conditions is accepted in some contexts, such as withdrawing life support from the terminally ill, and under debate in other conditions, such as allowing newborns to starve to death when a decision has been made not to operate on Down Syndrome babies with intestinal obstructions.

The official American Medical Association position, quoted at the beginning of this chapter, condemns active euthanasia but permits passive euthanasia, especially the withholding of extraordinary means or heroic measures from the patient. I will criticize the logic of this distinction and the AMA position later, but first we should look at some cases that illustrate the various positions.

Cases of voluntary passive euthanasia happen every day. When a doctor respects the wishes of a Jehovah's Witness or Christian Scientist practitioner and refrains from giving the believer a life-saving blood transfusion, the doctor is practicing passive voluntary euthanasia. When the doctor withdraws a life support machine from a patient in a persistent vegetative state or a seriously defective neonate, or refuses to use extraordinary means to save these patients' lives, he or she is practicing involuntary passive euthanasia. In the case of the Korean woman described in the previous chapter, the doctors finally acceded to her wishes and removed the life support system, so that she died. In the case of permanently comatose patients, like Karen Ann Quinlan and Nancy Cruzon, lawyers and doctors argued whether it was right to practice passive involuntary euthanasia and withdraw the life support system.

A most interesting case regarding voluntary passive euthanasia is the famous "Texas burn case" in which a young, athletic man, Donald C., was terribly burned when a gas line exploded, leaving 68 percent of his body burnt. Crippled, left blind, and without fingers, he was kept alive in the hospital, against his will, for 2 years by a series of painful treatments. Donald continually demanded to be left alone to die, but his doctors refused to allow him to die. A psychiatrist examined him and found him perfectly rational.

Should Donald C. have been allowed to die? He is alive today and glad of it. But he believes that his right to die was violated, and if he ever was to go through that ordeal again, he would want to be left to die.

Is he right? Can life become so burdensome, so filled with pain and suffering, that it loses all meaning and value?

Cases of active euthanasia are even more controversial than those of passive euthanasia, for they involve doing something positive to induce death.

In March 1983 Johanna Florian of Fort Lauderdale, Florida, was suffering from the irreversible condition Alzheimer's disease, along with thyroid problems, that would eventually make her senile and helpless. Her husband, Hans, couldn't stand to see his wife suffer and degenerate, so one Friday the 79-year-old Hans lifted Johanna from her hospital bed, wheeled her into the stairwell, and fatally shot her in the head. When the nurse rushed in and saw what had happened, she ordered Hans back into his wife's room. "The old man meekly obeyed." He was later charged with first-degree murder.[4]

Hans Florian had broken the law and murdered his wife, but had he done anything morally wrong? The Florida grand jury refused to indict him.

R. M. Hare tells the story of a truck driver whose truck had turned over and who lay pinned under the cabin while the truck was on fire. The driver, who was slowly roasting away, begged the onlookers to hit him on the head so that he would not roast to death. Should they have done so as they watched the man slowly die in agony?[5]

The celebrated journalist Stewart Alsop relates an incident that took place in the early 1970s while he was a patient in the solid tumor ward of the cancer clinic of the National Institutes of Health in Bethesda, Maryland. His roommate was a 28-year-old man he called Jack. Jack had a malignant tumor in his stomach about the size of a softball, which had metastasized and was beyond control.

Jack was in constant pain. His doctors prescribed an intravenous shot of a synthetic opiate every 4 hours, but it was impossible to control the pain that long. After a few hours Jack would begin to moan or whimper, "then he would begin to howl like a dog." A nurse would come. Codeine would then be given, but it usually did little good, and Jack continued in agony.

"The third night of this routine," Alsop writes, "the terrible thought occurred to me, 'If Jack were a dog . . . what would be done with him?' The answer was obvious: the pound and chloroform. No human being with a spark of pity could let a living thing suffer so, to no good end."[6]

There are essentially four arguments against voluntary active euthanasia. Probably the oldest argument against it is the argument from Natural Law. Active euthanasia violates Natural Law. We have a natural inclination to preserve life, which is trespassed in this act. We have already commented on this argument in discussing suicide. The notion of Natural Law can't be used to argue against either suicide or euthanasia. Medicine itself would be prohibited if we only followed the natural course of things. Certainly we wouldn't build airplanes or dams. Just as we use a dam to divert a river from its course to prevent flooding of a city, so it seems natural to use a knife to divert a few pints of blood from reaching the brain to release a terminally ill patient from a period of hopeless suffering.

The second argument is that voluntary active euthanasia is "playing God" and violates the sanctity of life. Only God is allowed to take an innocent life. Our right to life cannot be waived.

The use of the term "playing God" is just a pejorative way of emoting against autonomous action. To use medicine to keep a sick person from dying is playing God, if playing God means affecting the prospects of death. To kill harmful bacteria is to play God. Defending one's self from a rapist by killing him is playing God. Using birth control devices is playing God, as is feeding the starving or administering population control programs. All difficult moral decisions involve the kind of reasoning and action that might be labeled "playing God."

If playing God simply means doing what will affect the chances of life and death, then a lot of responsible social action does that. If, on the other hand, the term means unwarrantedly affecting the life chances of someone, then the question boils down to what is morally correct behavior in dealing with the dying process. What we need to know is which types of playing God are morally correct and which are not.

Sometimes the argument against playing God can be reduced to the property argument discussed in the previous chapter. We are stewards of God's property, so we may not mishandle it or throw it away by killing it. But, of course, we are responsible for using our reason in handling God's property. We do take lives in self-defense, so why not in self-defense against torture or great and irreversible suffering? The best way to exercise stewardship with God's property is to use the best reasons available in using it. Sometimes that will mean dispensing with it, especially when it is doing great harm.

Next comes the Slippery Slope argument—if we allow active euthanasia, it will lead to terrible abuses. Here is how former President Ronald Reagan's speech writer, Patrick Buchanan, put it.[7]

> Once we embrace this utilitarian ethic—that Man has the sovereign right to decide who is entitled to life and who is not—we have boarded a passenger train on which there are no scheduled stops between here and Birkenau.
>
> Once we accept that there are certain classes—i.e., unwanted unborn children, unwanted infants who are retarded or handicapped, etc.—whose lives are unworthy of legal protection, upon what moral high ground do we stand to decry when Dr. Himmler slaps us on the back, and asks us if he can include Gypsies and Jews?

The Slippery Slope argument is weak. Although the sentiments expressed in Mr. Buchanan's passage are to be taken seriously, the argument is invalid. Just because a practice *can be abused* does not entail that it shouldn't be used at all. Salt and sugar can be abused and harm us, but that doesn't mean that they shouldn't be used at all—even for legitimate purposes. Knives, cars, and drugs can be abused, but that doesn't mean that they should be outlawed.

We can well imagine serious abuses of the right to die. Imagine Aunt Ann dying of cancer. She is running up a large hospital and doctor bill, so that her savings are being depleted. Now Nephew Ned, who figures to collect handsomely from Aunt Ann's estate, is certain that Aunt Ann would be better off dead than alive. He encourages Aunt Ann to come to the same conclusion before her estate becomes bankrupt. We would want to take measures against such manipulation, but if we became convinced that we could not control them, we might well concede that voluntary active euthanasia, while in principle moral, should not become legal.

Difficult as it may be, we can safeguard terminally ill patients from most manipulative practices, so that the Slippery Slope argument isn't obviously valid here. The lesson of the argument is to get us to take measures that will protect patients from abuse.

Finally, those opposed to active euthanasia often appeal to the difference between "killing" and "letting die," so that while passive euthanasia may sometimes be justified, it doesn't follow that active euthanasia is. A fundamental difference exists between *doing* something and *allowing* something to happen. This is a standard attack on voluntary active euthanasia. It is the argument included in the AMA statement cited at the beginning of this chapter.

But is there really is a fundamental difference between killing and letting die, between active and passive euthanasia? First of all, it isn't clear that letting something bad happen is always worse (or more morally culpable) than *doing* something bad.

Judith Jarvis Thomson gives the following counterexample to this dogma. John is a trolley driver who suddenly realizes that his brakes have failed. He is heading for a group of workers on the track before him and will certainly kill them if something isn't done immediately. Fortunately, there is a side track to the right onto which John can turn the trolley. Unfortunately, there is one worker on that track who will be killed if John turns the trolley.

Now if the passive–active distinction holds, John should do nothing but simply allow the trolley to take its toll of the five men on the track before him. But that seems terrible. Surely, by turning quickly and causing the trolley to move onto the right track John will be saving a total of four lives. Most of us think that he should turn the trolley to the right and actively cause the death of one man rather than passively allow the death of the five. John is caught in a situation in which he cannot help doing or allowing harm, but he can act so that the lesser of the evils obtains—rather than the greater of the evils. Sometimes, we have a duty actively to cause evil rather than permit a greater evil. This may be part of the justification of a just war. Better to enter the war against the Nazi regime, and thus cause the death of many people, than allow it to triumph over innocent people.

This shows that the passive–active distinction doesn't always have the moral significance that it seems to have. Actively harming is not always worse than passively allowing to harm. Consider the following illustration offered by James Rachels.[8]

Smith stands to gain a large inheritance if anything should happen to his 6 -year-old cousin. One evening while the child is taking his bath, Smith sneaks into the bathroom and drowns the child, and then arranges things so that it will look like an accident. No one is the wiser, and Smith gets his inheritance.

Jones also stands to gain if anything should happen to his 6 -
year-old cousin. Like Smith, Jones sneaks in planning to drown the
child in his bath. However, just as he enters the bathroom Jones sees
the child slip, hit his head, and fall face-down in the water. Jones is
delighted; he stands by, ready to push the child's head back under
if necessary, but it is not necessary. With only a little thrashing about,
the child drowns all by himself, 'accidentally,' as Jones watches and
does nothing. No one is the wiser, and Jones gets his inheritance.

Is there really any difference between the moral culpability of Smith
and Jones? Is Jones's behavior less reprehensible than Smith's? From a
legal point of view, Smith is guilty of first-degree murder, whereas Jones
is not, but from a moral point of view these acts seem identical. Both
acted from identical motives (personal greed) and both had the same
end in view (the death of the child). The result is also the same: the
child, who Smith and Jones were responsible for saving, died.

Philosophers like Rachels take this argument to show that sometimes
there is no morally significant difference between killing and letting die.
What counts is our motives in doing what we do and the kind of
deliberation that goes into our acts. If Rachels is correct, then the AMA
policy, *that while passive euthanasia is permissible, active euthanasia is always
forbidden,* is itself incoherent.

Some people object that arguments like Rachels's against the passive–active distinction miss the point of the AMA guideline. According to
the ethicists Paul Ramsey and Thomas Sullivan, what is crucial in the
AMA statement is the difference between using ordinary and extraordinary means of preserving life. Here is how Ramsey puts it[9]:

> Ordinary means of preserving life are all medicines, treatments, and
> operations, which offer a reasonable hope of benefit for the patient
> and which can be obtained and used without excessive expense,
> pain and other inconveniences.
>
> Extra-ordinary means of preserving life are all those medicines,
> treatments, and operations which cannot be obtained without
> excessive expense, pain, or other inconveniences, or which, if used,
> would not offer a reasonable hope of benefit.

The idea is that we don't have to keep people alive at all costs. This
is correct, but it ignores the question of whether the terminally ill person
has a right to die and to be assisted to die.

But another distinction is embedded in this argument: the difference between intending to kill someone and foreseeing that he or she
will die. The woman who is attacked and raped as she walks through a
dangerous neighborhood at night to get home doesn't intend to get

raped, though she foresees the possibility and takes her chances. The pilot who drops bombs on enemy installations foresees that innocent people will be killed by his bombs but doesn't intend for them to die. Likewise, the doctor who refuses to use high-level technology to extend a terminally ill patient's life merely foresees that the patient will die. He doesn't intend for the patient to die.

This argument misses the point, confusing intention with action. An act may be morally correct but brought about by a bad intention, or it may be immoral but brought about by a good intention. For example, Jones and Smith both give $1000 to a worthy cause, but whereas Jones is concerned for the welfare of the people who will be helped by his donation, Smith gives to gain a good reputation. The same act, but two different intentions. Or conversely, Jones and Smith give the donation to help a terrorist cause. Jones gives because he is misguided (culpably, let us say), whereas Smith gives simply for the prestige he will gain by so giving. In this case the same wrong act is accompanied by a good motive (Jones) and a bad one (Smith).

The point is that an act is good or bad independent of whether the motive or intention is good or bad. The intention speaks eloquently of the person's character, but it doesn't touch on the value of the act in question.

If this is correct then the intention–foresight distinction is largely irrelevant to problems of euthanasia. What is primarily at issue is not the intention of the physician (it is hoped that will be good) but the objective rightness of terminating a life where the reasons to do so are good.

It is not enough to see that the arguments against euthanasia are weak. We want to see what can be said positively in its favor. There are three arguments that support it: The Right-to-Life Argument, The Golden Rule Argument, and The Combined Argument from Freedom and Prevention of Cruelty.

1. The Right to Life includes the Right to Die.   If I have a right to live my life as I see fit, then as long as I am not harming others, I can do what I like with my life, including waive that right and put myself to death. But if I cannot put myself to death without another's help, then the other person has a duty to assist in my death. This assisted death is called *allocide* (from the Greek *allo* —"other"—and the Latin *cide* —"death"). When it involves a terminally ill patient, we designate it active euthanasia. So in cases where I need help, my right to live may entail a right to be helped by another to die.

This argument is partially correct. If I have any right at all it is the right to do with my own life what I see fit, including ending my life, so long as I do not unjustly violate any other person's rights. The argument is too strong, however, in asserting that my right to die entails that other people have a duty to assist me in my death. Just as a right to drive a car does not entail that my neighbors have to buy me a car if I can't afford one, so a right to die does not entail that others have a duty to assist me in my death. Whether they have a weak duty may depend on our relationship, expectations, and promises as well as their feelings about suicide. This right-to-life/right-to-die argument only grants one a right to take one's own life. It doesn't by itself entail allocide or euthanasia.

2. The Golden Rule Argument.   The Golden Rule states that we should do unto others as we would have others do unto us (if we were in their shoes). If I was the driver under the burning truck, I would want someone to kill me swiftly in order that I not roast to death. So I should kill the truck driver before me. Of course, this sense of duty could be overridden by the thought that I may go to jail for several years for voluntary manslaughter. But if we waive that threat, then the Golden Rule seems to advise us to kill people who are being tortured by pain and who have no hope of remission.

3. The Combined Argument from Freedom and the Prevention of Cruelty.   Two of the basic values of a civilized society are freedom and the elimination of cruelty or unnecessary suffering. Maximal freedom or autonomy consistent with the freedom of others is a desideratum, a fundamental value. Likewise, if civilized people abhor anything, it is cruelty. The sadist or torturer calls up our deepest disdain and condemnation. But a suffering person, like Jack (in Stewart Alsop's story) or the immolated truck driver (in R. M. Hare's story) or Mrs. C, the Korean woman (in my story), is being tortured by nature. Freedom dictates that we allow them to choose whether they want to die sooner and without pain, and the principle of preventing cruelty dictates that we do whatever necessary to help them die.

You must decide whether these arguments are convincing. If they are correct, then society's present thinking about suicide and euthanasia is superstitious or, at least, confused. Even if you agree that euthanasia is morally permissible, this in itself does not entail that it should be *legally* permissible. Not every moral principle should be incorporated into law (for example, principles forbidding lying and bad intentions couldn't effectively be enforced). The consequences of legalizing euthanasia could be sufficiently bad as to prevent us from making the act legal. One could imagine nephew Johnny, who stands to inherit a largesse from Aunt Anny, encouraging his dear old aunt to leave this life "for the greater good" of all concerned. "Aunty, you seem to be losing your health and energy. Life must be a burden for you."

On the other hand, in general the laws should reflect these moral concerns, and safeguards should be built into the law to prevent abuse of a legitimate but dangerous practice.

Until the present laws are changed, each person should have a living will to ensure that he or she will not be kept alive (receive extraordinary measures) against his or her will. A typical living will looks like this[10]:

A LIVING WILL

Death is as much a reality as maturity and old age—it is one certainty of life. If the time comes when I, _____ , can no longer take part in decisions for my own future, let this statement stand as an expression of my wishes, while I am still of sound mind.

If the situation should arise in which there is no reasonable expectation of my recovery from physical or mental disability, I request that I be allowed to die and not be kept alive by artificial means or "heroic measures." I do not fear death itself as much as the indignities of deterioration, dependence, and hopeless pain. I, therefore, ask that medication be mercifully administered to me to alleviate suffering even though this may hasten the moment of death.

This request is made after careful consideration. I hope you who care for me will feel morally bound to follow its mandate. I recognize that this appears to place a heavy responsibility upon you, but it is with the intention of relieving you of such responsibility and of placing it upon myself in accordance with my strong conviction that this statement is made.

Study Questions

1. Outline the differences between the four forms of euthanasia. Which types do you think are morally permissible? Which are not?

2. Discuss the case of Janet Adkins (from the Introduction to this book). Was she right in wanting to end her life? Was Dr. Kevorkian morally correct in assisting her (allocide)? Should the situation have been dealth with differently?

3. Discuss the case of Karen Ann Quinlan. What decisions, if any, do you disagree with? Why:

4. Discuss the AMA position (mentioned at the beginning of this chapter) regarding passive and active euthanasia. Does Rachel's

counterexample undermine that distinction? Does the trolley car example show that something is wrong with the distinction?

5. Do you think that the right to live entails a right to die under certain circumstances? Explain.

6. Should the laws be changed to legalize active voluntary euthanasia?

Endnotes

1. Gregory Pence, *Classic Cases in Medical Ethics* (New York: McGraw-Hill, 1990), p. 11.

2. Quoted in Ibid, p. 13.

3. *The New York Times*, June 26, 1990.

4. Knight-Ridder Newspapers, March 19, 1983.

5. R. M. Hare, *Philosophic Exchange* vol. II. (Summer 1975), p. 45. Hare continues: "Now will you please all ask yourselves, as I have many times asked myself, what you wish that men should do to you if you were in the situation of the driver. I cannot believe that anybody who considered the matter seriously, as if he himself were going to be in that situation and had now to give instructions as to what rule the bystanders should follow, would say that the rule should be one ruling out euthanasia absolutely."

6. Stewart Alsop, "The Right to Die with Dignity," *Good Housekeeping* (August 1974), p. 130.

7. Patrick Buchanan, *Birmingham News*, November 16, 1983, p. 11a; quoted in James Rachels, *The End of Life* (Oxford: Oxford University Press, 1986), p. 63.

8. Ibid, p. 112.

9. Paul Ramsey, *The Patient as Person*, quoted in Thomas Sullivan, "Active and Passive Euthanasia: An Impertinent Distinction?" *Human Life Review* vol. III, no. 3 (Summer 1977), p. 44.

10. Copies and information are available from The Society for the Right to Die, 250 W. 57th St, New York, NY 10107.

Interlude:
On the Use and Abuse of Slippery Slope Arguments in Moral Arguments

The legal scholar, Yale Kamisar, echoes the fears of many people when he argues that we ought not to permit voluntary euthanasia of terminally ill patients since such a practice may bring us closer to involuntary euthanasia.[1] The moral theologian Joseph V. Sullivan puts it this way[2]:

> To permit in a single instance the direct killing of an innocent person would be to admit a most dangerous wedge that might eventually put all life in a precarious condition. Once a man is permitted on his own authority to kill an innocent person directly, there is no way of stopping the advancement of that wedge. There exists no longer any rational grounds for saying that the wedge can advance so far and no further. Once the exception has been made it is too late; hence the grave reason why no exception may be allowed. That is why euthanasia under any circumstances must be condemned.
>
> If voluntary euthanasia were legalized, there is good reason to believe that at a later date another bill for compulsory euthanasia would be legalized. Once respect for human life is so low that an innocent person may be killed directly even at his own request, compulsory euthanasia will necessarily be very near. This could lead easily to killing all incurable charity patients, the aged who are a public care, wounded soldiers, all deformed children, the mentally afflicted, and so on. Before long the danger would be at the door of every citizen.

Others have argued that if we legalize abortion (except possibly to save the mother's life), we embark on a course leading to infanticide and, eventually, the killing of small children and unwanted elderly.

Robert Wright argues in a similar vein on behalf of animal rights. "Once you buy the premise that animals can experience pain and pleasure, and that their welfare therefore deserves *some* consideration, you're on the road to comparing yourself with a lobster. There may be some exit ramps along the way—plausible places to separate welfare from rights—but I can't find any."[3]

Perhaps nowhere is the Slippery Slope argument used more effectively than in the abortion debate. Opponents of abortion, like John Noonan, argue that since there is no nonarbitrary cutoff point between conception of the single-cell zygote and the full adult where we can say, "Here we do not have a human being and here we do," to draw the line anywhere but at conception is to justify infanticide, the killing of small children, and the unwanted elderly.[4]

Where do you draw a nonarbitrary line in these social practices? Slippery Slope arguments, sometimes called *Edge of the Wedge* arguments, have been used as the trump card of traditionalists opposed to social change. Give innovation an inch and it will take a mile. The first step to Auschwitz begins with a seemingly innocent concession to those who would promote social considerations over the sanctity of life.

Let's examine these kinds of arguments. But first I want to prove to you that no poor people exist in the world. You will agree that having a single penny does not make the difference between being wealthy or poor, won't you? Perhaps having a penny will make the difference in purchasing something, but that in itself doesn't constitute the difference between poverty and wealth. Then I hope that you'll agree that possessing a billion dollars constitutes being wealthy (it used to be only a million dollars, but such is inflation and the sliding notion of comparative wealth). Now take a penny away from our billionaire. Does the loss of one cent make him poor? Of course not. We've already agreed that the gain or loss of one penny doesn't make a difference with regard to whether someone is poor or wealthy. Now take another penny from him and another and another until he only is worth $1.25, the price of the Sunday *New York Times*. He's homeless and can't even afford a half-gallon of milk, but by our argument, he's not poor, for all we did was subtract pennies from him one by one and such small increments can't make a difference.

Of course, we could work the argument the other way around and prove that no one is rich—that everyone is poor. We'll agree to the same crucial premise that a penny doesn't make a difference between wealth and poverty. Then we'll agree that possessing only a penny makes no one rich. Then we'll add a penny to our poor man, one by one, until he possesses a hundred billion pennies or a billion dollars.

Or consider this argument. No one is really bald, for taking a single hair from anyone with a complete head of hair cannot produce baldness, so we begin to take hairs from your head one by one until you have no hair at all on your head. At what point were you really bald? Surely, having one piece of hair is being bald, and adding a second makes no difference to the designation of being bald. So we can go from baldness to a full head of hair without ever finding a cutoff point where baldness ends and hairiness begins. Yet we are sure that there is a difference between baldness and a full scalp.

When does an accumulation of sand, soil, and rock become a mountain? A piece of sand, a speck of soil, and a tiny stone do not constitute a mountain, but if we keep adding sand, soil, and rocks long enough we'll eventually end up with a structure larger than Mt. Everest!

You get the point. Concepts are clear. Their application in reality is unclear. The Slippery Slope arguments trade on this vagueness. The fallacy of the Slippery Slope argument is to suppose that because there is no distinct cutoff point in reality where concepts change (rich to poor, etc.), there is no real difference between state A and state B. But there is. We know the difference between wealth and poverty even though we cannot define it in absolute monetary terms. We know the difference between a full head of hair and baldness even though we cannot say exactly where baldness begins. We know the difference between a hill and a mountain even though there is a grey area in between where we're not sure what to call it.

The lesson of vagueness is to remind us, transposing Hegel's dictum, that "while concepts are green life is grey." We ought to be careful in making social policy, and we ought to guard against abuse. Where there is doubt, we ought to err on the side of protecting life.

Now apply this point to the moral dilemmas discussed in this book. There may be grounds for permitting abortion at early stages of development, whereas we want to protect self-conscious human life. Even though we do not know where the line is drawn (no line may exist), it doesn't mean that no difference exists. The lesson of the Slippery Slope kind of reasoning is to play it safe, to err on the side of life. So since there is no definite cutoff point where mere biologic life ends and self-conscious life begins, we'll pick a safe place within the grey area.

Likewise with euthanasia. We should set safeguards for the innocent so that ruthless relatives hoping to gain an early inheritance can't exploit Aunt Anny by granting her a blessed exit into the beyond.

And likewise with our animal rights argument. Just because we recognize an animal's ability to experience pleasure and pain as morally significant doesn't mean that we are forbidden to call the exterminator when termites are devouring our houses, or that we can't eat animals or experiment on animals for human good. We must be able to justify our practices in impartial ways. As far as we know chickens, termites, and experimental mice do not have a notion of self and do not reason in self-conscious ways, so that killing them is not violating their right to carry out personal projects in the same way as if we killed our fellow humans or self-conscious chimpanzees.

Where and how to draw the line is a difficult problem, and we may err, but part of the human condition is to be called upon to make difficult decisions and take responsibility for the consequences. This is the essence of moral reasoning—to reason impartially, to change your mind as the evidence refutes you, and to take responsibility for your actions. This is dangerous, but it's also challenging and calls on the best that is in us.

One more point must made. The Reverse Slippery Slope argument can be maintained to justify social change: If we don't act justly in this small issue, we may be hardened so that we won't act justly in a large issue. Unless we grant women the right to abortion and terminally ill people the right to die, all of our rights may be in jeopardy.

The Reverse Slippery Slope argument, while an exaggeration, is as good as the basic version of the argument.

Endnotes

1. Yale Kamisar, "Euthanasia Legislation: Some Nonreligious Objections," *Minnesota Law Review* vol. 42, no. 6 (1958).

2. Joseph V. Sullivan, "The Immortality of Euthanasia," in Marvin Kohl, ed., *Beneficent Euthanasia* (Buffalo: Prometheus, 1975), p. 24.

3. Robert Wright, "Are Animals People Too?" *New Republic* (March 12, 1990).

4. John T. Noonan, "An Almost Absolute Value in History," reprinted in Joel Feinberg, ed., *The Problem of Abortion* (Belmont, Calif.: Wadsworth, 1984).

CHAPTER 6

Abortion: *The Greatest Moral Problem of our Generation*

*Every unborn child must be regarded as a human person with all
the rights of a human person, from the moment of conception.*

—ETHICAL AND RELIGIOUS DIRECTIVES FOR CATHOLIC HOSPITALS

*[Abortion] during the first two or three months of gestation [is
morally equivalent] to removal of a piece of tissue from the
woman's body.*

—THOMAS SZASZ, "THE ETHICS OF ABORTION," *HUMANIST*, 1966

*With reference to [Abortion] the world is upside down. When a
criminal is sentenced to death, the whole world is dismayed
because it goes against human rights. But when an unborn baby
is sentenced to death, the world approves of it because the
"rights" of the mother take precedence over the rights of an
innocent human life. But how is this different from the Nazi
holocaust where Mother Germany sent twelve million innocent
lives to the gas chamber? Haven't we sent over 30 million
innocent lives to their death?*

—LOIS HOPE WALKER

INTRODUCTION: GENOCIDE
OR EXPRESSION OF AUTONOMY?

The major social issue that divides our society as no other issue does is the
moral and legal status of the human fetus and the corresponding

question of the moral permissibility of abortion. On the one hand, such organizations as the Roman Catholic Church and the Right-to-Life Movement, appalled by the more than 1.5 million abortions that take place in the United States each year, have exerted significant political pressure toward introducing a constitutional amendment that would grant full legal rights to fetuses. These movements have made abortion the single issue in recent political campaigns. On the other hand, prochoice groups, such as The National Organization of Women (NOW), the National Abortion Rights Action League (NARAL), and feminist organizations, have exerted enormous pressure on politicians to support pro-abortion legislation. The Republican and Democratic political platforms of the past two elections (1984 and 1988) took diametrically opposite sides on this issue.

Let's look at the argument of Lois Hope Walker. Imagine we're in Nazi Germany in 1943. Millions of Jews, gypsies, retarded people, and protestors are being sent to the gas chambers. Are we doing the same today to millions of innocent fetuses? And are those who countenance today's behavior similar to those who looked the other way as the Jews were led to Auschwitz, Dachau, Bergen-Belsen, Birchenau, and Treblinka? This is how the antiabortionist regards our present practice of abortion.

Note that the same arguments used to justify abortion could be used to justify the holocaust: (1) A woman has an absolute right to do what she wants with her own body = Mother Germany has an absolute right to do what she likes with her body, the German people. (2) Fetuses are not fully human = the Jews and retarded people are not fully human. (3) If we don't make abortion legal, women will seek abortions anyway and risk their lives = if we don't make destroying the Jews legal, the people will take the law into their own hands and risk their lives in eliminating the Jews.

In the 1988 Presidential Debate Michael Dukakis argued that a woman has an absolute right to have an abortion because she has an absolute right to her own body. President Bush responded by contending that because the fetus was a human being, abortion was an act of murder. This would also make the doctor who performed the abortion a murderer. I will examine each of these arguments in a moment. How you decide on the abortion issue has wide-ranging effects, including effects on a whole host of other political, legal, and moral questions.

Why is abortion a moral issue? Take a fertilized egg, a zygote, a tiny sphere of cells. By itself it is hard to see what is so important about such an inconspicuous piece of matter. It is virtually indistinguishable from other clusters of cells or zygotes of other animals. On the other hand, take an adult human being, a class of beings that we all intuitively feel to be worthy of high respect, having rights, including the right to life. To kill an innocent human being is an act of murder and universally condemned. However, no obvious line of division separates that single-cell zygote from the adult it will become. Whence, the problem of abortion.

I shall begin my examination by sketching the three main positions on abortion. I shall draw the implications from the major arguments on the two ends of the spectrum and then turn to the middle position, which seeks to make a compromise between the concerns of the other positions. The conservative position says that because fetuses are full human beings, abortion is never justified, except perhaps to save the mother's life. Perhaps the most developed version of the conservative position is that of the Roman Catholic Church, which allows abortion only in the cases of (1) ectopic pregnancy—when the embryo is lodged in the fallopian tube—and (2) a cancerous uterus, where the death of the fetus is *foreseen* but not *intended.*

John Noonan formulates the conservative argument this way:

1. We ought never to kill innocent human beings (except in self-defense when our lives are threatened).
2. Fetuses are innocent human beings.
3. Therefore, we ought never to kill fetuses—that is, have abortions (except in self-defense when the mother's life is threatened by the pregnancy).

The liberal position is that because the fetus is not a human being but has the same status as a vestigial organ, abortion is justified any time the woman desires to have an abortion.

Thomas Szasz's view that abortion during "the first two or three months of gestation [is morally equivalent] to removal of a piece of tissue from the woman's body," seems extreme, but it is frank and accurate. For the liberal the fetus has no more moral status than the appendix.

Moderates argue that a fetus does not have a full right to life, but as a potential person it has some rights, and abortion may be justified only in the earliest stages of pregnancy, or when the fetus promises to be seriously defective, or when the pregnancy constitutes a danger to the mother's health or life.

The debate usually starts with the question of when the fetus does become a full human being, a *person* with a right to life. Liberals traditionally say that a cutoff point occurs somewhere. Let us look at the proposed candidates for such a cutoff point.

1. Quickening. People used to maintain that the soul entered the body at quickening, and some theologians countenanced abortion during the first weeks of pregnancy on the basis that the fetus had not yet been ensouled. Few still hold this view, since quickening is merely the first experience of the mother feeling the fetus move.

2. *Viability*. The United States Supreme Court in the *Roe v. Wade* (1973) decision came close to espousing viability as the cutoff point between not having a right to life and having one. The court held that the state has a legitimate interest in protecting potential life and that this interest becomes compelling at viability "because the fetus then presumably has the capability of meaningful life, outside the mother's womb." But the judgment lacks adequate argumentative support. It doesn't tell us why the life of a 6-month- old fetus is more meaningful outside the womb than inside, nor why the viable fetus has more potential human life than the not-yet-viable fetus. One would think that the potentiality was relatively similar.

Another criticism is that the viability criterion makes humanness dependent on the state of technology. Thirty years ago little Johnny who is a 6-month- old fetus would have been a nonperson, but today, thanks to technology, he is judged a full person. It seems odd to base the metaphysical issue of personhood on the whims and caprice of technology. A fetus either has intrinsic value or it doesn't. Something external, like medical technology, doesn't affect that value. Personhood is more than a matter of luck.

3. *Experience*. A being with a right to life must be able to perceive, suffer, and remember. The fetus cannot do any of these things, so it is not a full human being. This argument seems dubious for three reasons. First, the criterion, strictly interpreted, would exclude infants from being persons since they do not perceive in the strong sense of that term, nor do they remember. But secondly, in the weak sense of experience there is some evidence that fetuses can suffer pain and pleasure, "experience" sensations, and so forth. Furthermore, the criterion could be used to give animals (including insects) equal rights to life, for they also experience.

4. *Birth*. Many people hold that birth is the decisive cutoff point between nonpersonhood and personhood. But this seems an arbitrary distinction. There is no reason to suppose that the fetus's status one second before birth is miraculously transformed one second after birth. A prematurely born infant may actually be less developed than a fetus near the end of a normal pregnancy. Birth is simply the time when the baby is detached from the mother's body and becomes a visible social being. It has no intrinsic significance. If children stayed attached to the mother's placenta or large mechanical incubators (perish the thought) until they were 10 years old, they wouldn't suddenly become human beings on being detached.

The conclusion is that neither quickening, viability, experience, nor birth are nonarbitrary cutoff points between nonhumanness and humanness. So there doesn't seem to be a cutoff point between conception and infancy. If there is not, then either single-cell zygotes are full human beings with a right to life or else infants are not full human beings with a right to life. Since most liberals and moderates are horrified by the thought of viewing infanticide as morally acceptable, they are defeated. The conservative wins the debate.

But if the conservative wins, he or she must pay a high price for victory. If all forms of human life are equally valuable and grant the being, whether it be a fetus or an adult, an equal right to life, radical consequences follow. In particular, there is no reason to prefer the mother's life to the fetus's when the two are in conflict. In fact, there is reason to save the fetus instead of the mother. Three arguments support this thesis.

1. The Fairness Argument.   If life is the highest value, we ought to sacrifice the mother for the fetus because the mother has already enjoyed a number of years but the fetus hasn't. It should be given its turn.

2. The Self-Defense Argument.   You may counter that the mother has a right to defend herself against the fetus, for we have a right to defend our lives against those who threaten it even if those who threaten it are innocent. That may be, but then isn't the doctor, who performs the abortion, acting as an accomplice in a killing? By what right does he take sides? Wouldn't the doctor be at least as justified in preferring the life of the fetus? If the fetus is a full human, doesn't it deserve legal representation?

3. The Invited Guest Argument.   Assuming that the fetus was conceived in a voluntary act of sexual intercourse, isn't its presence similar to that of an invited guest in your home? When your roof begins to cave in, aren't you obligated to do everything in your power to save the guest even if it means risking your own life?

So if the conservative is correct in asserting that the fetus is a full human being, he or she cannot prefer the mother's life to the fetus's life when the two are in conflict.

Another implication of the conservative thesis is that rape is not a grounds for abortion. If all human life is of equal value, then no amount of mental suffering on the part of a teenager who has been brutally raped can justify our killing the fetus. The conservative reasons thusly: how grimly ironic and grossly illogical that people who are against capital punishment for the criminal, the rapist, would advocate it for one of the innocent victims, the fetus.

The conservative position leaves many of us in a dilemma, for it tells us that our intuitions about preferring the mother's life to the fetus's and about permitting abortion in the case of rape are mistaken. Sometimes we must give up our intuitions for our principles, but sometimes our intuitions are signals that our principles are too rigid or unqualified. In any case, before we jettison those intuitions, we should take a look at the liberal and moderate positions on abortion.

THE LIBERAL POSITION

The liberal position asserts that it is always or almost always morally permissible for a woman to have an abortion. It allows abortion on demand. Four arguments for this position have been offered. They are:

1. Subjectivism: Radical Relativism
2. The Absolute Right to Privacy Argument (reproductive freedom)
3. The Quality of Life Argument (in cases of the probability of defective neonates)
4. The Personhood Argument

1. Subjectivism: Radical Relativism.   Abortion is a private matter into which the law should not enter. No one should be forced to have children. H. Schur in his book *Crimes without Victims* calls abortion a victimless crime. Unfortunately, he supplies no argument for his view that fetuses are nonpersons. Schur assumes that morality is merely a matter of individual choice. Who are we to judge?

But subjectivism is a dubious doctrine. If fetuses are persons, then isn't what we're doing tantamount to killing innocent people? Aren't we all engaged in mass killings? And isn't the killing of innocents to be condemned?

2. The Absolute Right to Privacy Argument.   The National Organization of Women and many radical feminists hold that since a woman has an absolute right to her own body, on which a fetus is dependent, she may do whatever is necessary to detach the fetus from her, including putting it to death.

The first problem with this argument is that it is unclear whether we have any *absolute* rights at all. An absolute right is one that always overrides all other considerations. It is doubtful whether we have many of these. The only ones I can think of are rights such as the right not to be harmed or tortured unnecessarily. We have no reason to believe that our right to use our own body as we wish is an absolute right. Consider 500-lb. Fat Fred who decides to sit down, but your money-packed wallet happens to be directly on the spot where he sits. You request him to move his carcass so that you can get your wallet, but he refuses, claiming that he has an absolute right to do with his body what he wills.

The doctrine of absolute rights to privacy or body use suffers from lack of intelligent support. Since our bodies are public and interact with other people's bodies and property, we need ways of adjudicating conflicts between them, but there is no such thing as an absolute right to do whatever we want with our bodies. The parent of dependent children doesn't have a right to remove his or her body to a different locale, abandoning the children. A man may be morally obligated to take his body to the Army recruitment center when his nation is in danger and the draft board picks his number.

Suppose that President Bush suddenly has a rare form of liver and double kidney failure, so that he needs to be plugged into a human being's kidneys and liver. The person will have to walk around with the President, sleep in his bed, and eat at his table for 9 months. One hundred people with the right kinds of kidneys and livers are rounded up and invited to participate in a lottery. One person, the loser, will get plugged in to the President. Each of the one hundred people will win $1000 for playing the game. You are one of the people invited to play. Would you play?

Most people asked, including myself, say that they would take the risk of playing the lottery. Once we agree to play we are obligated to accept the inconvenience if we lose. It would be absurd to back out, claiming an absolute right to privacy or bodily use.

The implications of the lottery game for abortion are obvious. Once people voluntarily engage in sex, they are engaged in the lottery game. Even if they use birth control devices, pregnancy might result. If the fetus is a person with a right to life, the woman cannot simply dismiss that right by invoking a superior right to privacy. She has suspended that right by engaging in an act that brought the new being into existence.

3. The Quality of Life Argument.   One strategy available to the liberal is to deny that life is of absolute value. We set forth this argument in Chapter 2, arguing against the doctrine of the sanctity of life. The quality of life, not its quantity, is the crucial factor. Some lives are not worth living; they do not have positive value. The severely deformed, retarded, or hydrocephalic child may live a negative existence, in which case abortion may be warranted. Or suppose that a pregnant woman is informed that the fetus she is carrying has Tay–Sachs disease or spina bifida and is told that if she aborts, in 5 months she will be able to conceive a normal child. If it is quality that counts, the woman not merely may abort, but she has a positive duty to do so.

This argument can be extended to cover cases where the woman is incapable of providing an adequate upbringing for the child to be born, the case of the teenage pregnancy, the family with children that cannot afford another child. That the world is already overpopulated is another consideration arguing for abortion of unwanted children. No unwanted child should enter the world.

There is merit in the Quality of Life argument—quality does count—but it has weaknesses that must to be met. First, the argument against bringing unwanted children into the world may be offset by the availability of adoption. Many childless couples *want* these children. Nevertheless, not all children are likely to be adopted into loving homes, so that some abortions would still be permitted in a percentage of cases.

A more significant objection is that the Quality of Life argument leaves the status of the fetus untouched. If the fetus is a person, then it makes no more sense to speak of aborting it because you don't think it will have an adequate quality of life than it does to kill a baby or 10-year-old or 90-year-old because you don't think he or she will have an adequate quality of life. While quality counts, we don't have the right to play God in this way with people's lives. It's too dangerous.

So the status of the fetus has to be addressed.

4. The Personhood Argument.   Our intuitions generally tell us that the fetus does not have the same moral status as the mother. Antiabortionists often base their conclusions on our religious heritage, but even there the case is ambiguous. While the notion of ensoulment argues for the personhood of the fetus, earlier Biblical ideas lend support for a distinction of status. For example, Exodus (21:22) says that if a man causes a woman to abort, he shall be punished, but if the woman's death follows, those responsible shall give "life for life, eye for eye, tooth for tooth." Furthermore, serious difficulties arise with viewing the single-cell zygote or the conceptus as a person, given the phenomenon of twining, which can take place up to the third week of pregnancy. If the embryo splits into two (or three, four, or more) embryos, does one person (soul) become two (or more)? How can personhood, with its characteristic of complete unity, be divided?

But it is not enough for liberals to point out problems in the conservative position. The liberal must go to the heart of the matter and attempt to dismantle the conservative arguments for the fetus's right to life. The central one is that offered by Noonan (above).

1. We ought never to kill innocent human beings.
2. Fetuses are innocent human beings.
3. Therefore, we ought never to kill fetuses—that is, have abortions.

The liberal points out that the term *human being* is used ambiguously in the argument. Note that sometimes by *human being* we have a biologic concept in mind, the species *Homo sapiens,* but that at other times we have a psychologic–moral concept in mind, someone with the characteristics of humans as we typically find them, characteristics such as rationality, freedom, and self-consciousness, which mark them off from other animals. In philosophy we sometimes use the word *person* to refer to this type of being. A person is someone who has an intrinsic right to life. If we apply this distinction to Noonan's argument, we see that it trades on this ambiguity.

In the first premise "human beings" refers to persons, while in the second it refers to *Homo sapiens.* The argument should read:

1. We ought never to kill innocent *persons.*
2. Fetuses are innocent *Homo sapiens.*
3. Therefore, we ought never to kill fetuses.

But this is an invalid argument, since it is not obvious that all *Homo sapiens* are persons.

The question is, by virtue of what characteristics does someone have a right to life? The liberal will point out that it is a form of prejudice, similar to racism, sexism, nationalism, religionism, and ethnocentricism, to prefer one species to another simply because it is your species or to grant someone a right simply because he or she is a member of a biologic group. Peter Singer in his work on animal rights calls this prejudice *speciesism.*

Speciesism violates the first principle of justice: treat equals equally and unequals unequally. Suppose it turned out that one ethnic group or gender on average made better musicians than other groups. It would still be unjust automatically to allow all and only members of that group to enter music school. Individuals have a right to be judged according to their ability, and so we would want to test individuals independently of ethnic group or gender to ascertain potential for musical performance.

What are the characteristics that give beings a right to life analogous to the characteristics that give candidates a right to enter music school? The liberal argues that certain properties that most adult humans have are the proper criteria for this distinction. These properties are intrinsically valuable traits that allow us to view ourselves as selves with plans and projects over time, properties such as self-consciousness and rationality. Both conservatives and liberals agree that these qualities are intrinsically good. The liberal, however, tries to draw out their implications: that our ability to make plans, to think rationally, and to have a self over time give us a special right to life.

It is this property of rational self-consciousness that distinguishes the average adult human from most of the animal kingdom. But not all humans have these qualities, while some animals may possess them.

Severely retarded children, anencephalic babies, severely senile adults, and people in persistent vegetative states do not possess those properties, while dolphins, whales, chimpanzees, apes, and even some dogs and pigs may possess them. The diagram below represents the relationship between humans and animals with regard to personhood.

If rational self-consciousness marks the criterion for having a right to life, then fetuses do not have a right to life, since they are neither rational nor self-conscious.

THE CONSERVATIVE RESPONSE
AND LIBERAL COUNTERRESPONSE

How do conservatives respond to this argument? First they point out two counterintuitive implications of the liberal position, and then they point out something missing that changes the liberal's logic.

If the personhood argument were followed, we would be permitted to kill unconscious and severely retarded and senile humans—even normal people when they sleep, for none of these have the required characteristics for personhood. The argument would also sanction infanticide, something that most liberals are loathe to allow. Finally, the argument ignores the fact that the fetus is a *potential* person, and potentiality for self-consciousness should be seen as granting a being similar rights as an actual person.

Poignant as these objections are, the liberal has a response available to each of them. Regarding the killing of the retarded and senile, the liberal would point out that most of these people still have an adequate amount of rationality and that it would be dangerous to put into practice a policy of doing away with all but the most obvious cases of loss of selfhood. With regard to those who sleep or are unconscious, they still have the capacity for rational self-consciousness, so that we may not kill them.

Here the liberal distinguishes between a *capacity* and *potentiality*.

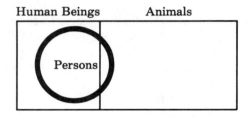

FIGURE 6-1

Consider a lump of clay. It doesn't have the capacity to hold water, but it has the potentiality for that capacity. Suppose that I mold it into a cup. Now it has the capacity for holding water even though at present it is not holding any. The fetus only has the potentiality for self-consciousness, whereas the unconscious person has the capacity for it.

Potentiality is not enough, only actuality or capacity for self-consciousness is sufficient for granting someone a right to life. Let me illustrate this with an example from the last presidential campaign. Suppose that during the campaign of the Democratic Party for the presidential nomination Jesse Jackson had suddenly appeared at the White House with his family and furniture. "I'm moving in here," he announces to an incredulous White House staff.

" You can't. It's unlawful!" objects the staff member.

" You don't know what you're talking about. Don't you Republicans believe that a potential person has all the rights of an actual person? Well, on that same logic, a potential president has the same rights as as actual president. Since I am potentially the president, I'm taking advantage of my rights, so let me in."

Although the fetus may be a potential person, it is not yet an actual one; hence, it does not have the same rights as an actual person.

We can cast greater doubt on this doctrine, for if someone believes that a single-cell zygote has a right to life, then he or she should refrain from washing and from brushing his or her teeth. Why? Because in doing so, that person is killing thousands of single cells *with exactly the same endowment* as the zygote. The primary difference between other diploid cells in our body and the zygote has to do with *activating* the potential latent chromosomal make up, not in the *essential* make up of the cell. But that is an irrelevant distinction, having nothing to do with the inherent worth or rights of the cell itself. Given the prospects of cloning, every cell in a blastocyst, and perhaps every cell in your body could be developed into a fetus, a baby, and, finally, into an adult. If the zygote is sacred and not to be destroyed, the same goes for every other human cell in the world.

Finally, liberals must respond to the objection that their view permits infanticide. In a sense it does, but it need not. Let me explain.

The liberal can distinguish between a natural right and a social right. A natural right is one a person has simply by virtue of intrinsic qualities. A social right, on the other hand, is not intrinsic to the being, but something bestowed by society. Society has the privilege of protecting things that it deems valuable or useful to its purposes. Just as it can grant a forest or an endangered animal species a protective right, so it can give fetuses or infants such rights if it so desires. The only condition for granting something a social right is that we give a utilitarian reason for doing so. Since the entity at issue doesn't have sufficient intrinsic value to demand the right, there must be an instrumental reason for doing so.

We are more willing to extend a social right to infants than to fetuses because they are closer to personhood and because they are independent of the mother's body and can be adopted. If a state decided that there were good reasons to extend the social right to life to fetuses, it would be justified in doing so. But it doesn't have to, and if there were good utilitarian reasons for doing so, the state could remove the social right to life from infants. Because the latter move would cause a revolt, this is unlikely to happen. Nonetheless, on the liberal argument, such a move could not be ruled out as morally unacceptable.

Let me set forth the above argument succinctly in eight steps so that you will be able to examine it carefully.

1. All and only actual persons have a moral *right* to life (that is, potentiality doesn't count).
2. Persons may be defined as beings who have the capacity for reason and self-conscious desire ("reason capacity").
3. Fetuses and infants do not have reason capacities and so do not have a moral right to life.
4. However, there are social rights (including the social right to life) which society may bestow on classes of beings for utilitarian reasons. This includes treating some potential persons as if they had the rights of persons.
5. There are good utilitarian reasons for treating viable fetuses (toward the end of the second trimester) and infants as persons, giving them social rights.
6. When in doubt, we ought to err on the side of life.
7. Therefore, we ought to bestow a social right on viable fetuses and infants (that is, once past a fixed time a woman loses her right to abort potential persons, except where they will be seriously defective or where the mother's life or health is endangered).
8. Therefore, we ought to allow abortion only in the earliest stages of pregnancy or when the fetus is known to be seriously defective, or else when the mother's life or health is endangered.

The core of the liberal position is the notion that we are not born persons but become such through adequate socialization. Becoming a person is not a biologic given but an interactive process. Studies by Bruno Bettleheim and others of children suffering severe forms of infantile autism (a form of childhood schizophrenia) show that infants abandoned or severely neglected by parents (even intelligent, educated, middle-class parents) fail to learn to speak and take on animal characteristics: eat raw meat, drink by lapping, tear their clothes off and prefer to run around naked, howl, growl at humans, and often bite those who attend them. Reports of feral children are controversial, but abandoned infants frequently take on wolflike traits. They lack language ability, lack a sense of self, and are unable to think abstractly.[1]

If *Homo sapiens* are not born persons but become such through a complex process of socialization, the liberal has grounds to permit abortion.

THE MODERATE POSITION

The moderate is caught in the middle of this controversy. He or she is dissatisfied with the arguments on both sides of the fence. Moderates object to the conservative prohibition of abortion because it is one-dimensional, seeing only the abstract right of the fetus and not the complications of life. The moderate contends against the conservative that the mother's psychologic condition and the quality of life of the fetus must be taken into consideration in deciding on abortion. A victim of rape, a pregnant 13-year-old, or a poor woman with too many children is probably justified in getting an abortion.

But the moderate doesn't agree with the liberal on the issue of abortion on demand. Fetuses are potential persons in a way that other single cells in the body are not. They are already in the process of developing into the kind of beings who will be socialized as self-conscious persons. The closer they come to birth, the more the presumption of life is in their favor.

Even though it is put forward by a conservative, John Noonan, the moderate is likely to accept the argument from probability.[2]

> Consider, for example, the spermatozoa in any normal ejaculate: There are about 200,000,000 in any single ejaculate, of which one has a chance of developing into a zygote. Consider the oocytes which may become ova: there are 100,000 to 1,000,000 oocytes in a female infant, of which a maximum of 390 are ovulated. But once spermatozoa and ovum meet and the conceptus is formed, such studies as have been made show that roughly in only 20 percent of the cases will spontaneous abortion occur. In other words, the chances are about 4 out of 5 that this new being will develop. At this stage in the life of the being there is a sharp shift in probabilities, an immense jump in potentialities. To make a distinction between the rights of spermatozoa and the rights of the fertilized ovum is to respond to an enormous shift in possibilities. For about twenty days after conception the egg may split to form twins or combine with another egg to form a chimera, but the probability of either event happening is very small.

Noonan's argument is one for moderatism because he is not arguing that biologic probabilities establish essential humanity, but simply that it is commonsensical to suppose that the fetus will develop into a person. As Noonan continues, "If the chance is 200,000,000 to 1 that the movement in the bushes into which you shoot is a man's, I doubt if many persons would hold you careless in shooting; but if the chances are 4 out of 5 that the movement is a human being's, few would acquit you of blame."

The argument from probability doesn't give the fetus a clear right to life, but it shows that there is a presumption against aborting. That is, a difference still stands between a potential person and an actual person, but since there is a high probability that the fetus will become a person, we should permit abortion only for compelling reasons, where the mother's health or life is endangered or where the quality of life of the fetus will be seriously compromised.

There you have the three positions and the significant arguments that attach to each one. You have a lot to sort out. If you are to work out a solution from a philosophic perspective, you need to give your reasons for preferring one position over the others. If you believe that an immortal soul inhabits the fetus from conception onward, you will be inclined toward some version of the conservative argument. If you believe that rational self-consciousness makes persons morally signifi-cant, then you will be inclined toward a version of the liberal position. If you believe that both sides have important considerations, you will be inclined toward the moderate perspective. Perhaps at this point you should read over the reason given in support of each position and weigh the comparative strengths of each major view. The crucial point is that you recognize the difficulty of the issue and use reason, rather than simply emotion, to work out your position.

Study Questions

1. Many people say, "I believe abortion is morally wrong, but I don't believe that there should be a law against it." Is this a coherent position? Is Lois Hope Walker right in comparing the killing of millions of fetuses to the killing of millions of people in Nazi concentration camps?

2. Evaluate the three basic positions: the Conservative, the Liberal, and the Moderate. What are the strengths and weaknesses of each? Which is the most cogent position? Why?

3. John Noonan draws the line between being nonhuman and being human at conception. Do you agree with his argument? Is conception an objectively based, nonarbitrary cutoff point between the two fundamental states?

4. Does the personhood argument that permits abortion also permit infanticide? Why don't those in favor of prochoice on abortion also advocate prochoice regarding infanticide?

5. Examine the moderate position based on the probability argument that a fetus very likely will develop into a full person. If it were adopted, would it cause us to change our social policy on abortion?

6. What is the relationship between a woman's autonomy and privacy and the responsibility to protect life?

Endnotes

1. See Bruno Bettleheim, "Feral Children and Autistic Children," *The American Journal of Sociology* 64 (March, 1959), pp. 455–467; and *The Empty Fortress: Infantile Autism and the Birth of the Self* (New York: The Free Press, 1967); see also George H. Mead, *Mind, Self and Society* (Chicago: University of Chicago Press, 1934).

2. John Noonan, "An Almost Absolute Value in History," in John Noonan, ed., *The Morality of Abortion: Legal and Historical Perspectives* (Cambridge: Harvard University Press, 1970), reprinted in Joel Feinberg, *The Problem of Abortion* (Belmont, Calif.: Wadsworth, 1984).

CHAPTER 7

The Death Penalty

To be sustained under the Eighth Amendment, the death penalty must [comport] with the basic concept of human dignity at the core of the Amendment; the objective in imposing it must be [consistent] with our respect for the dignity of [other] men. Under these standards, the taking of life "because the wrongdoer deserves it" surely must fail, for such a punishment has as its very basis the total denial of the wrongdoer's dignity and worth. The death penalty, unnecessary to promote the goal of deterrence or to further any legitimate notion of retribution, is an excessive penalty forbidden by the Eighth and Fourteenth Amendments.

—SUPREME COURT JUSTICE, THURGOOD MARSHALL,
GREGG V. GEORGIA, 1976

On August 15, 1990, Angel Diaz, age 19, was sentenced in the Bronx for the murder of an Israeli immigrant who had employed one of Diaz's friends. After strangling the man with a shoelace and stabbing him, Diaz and four friends donned Halloween masks to rob, beat, and gang-rape the man's wife and 16-year-old daughter. The women were then sexually tortured while the murdered man's 3-year-old daughter watched from her crib.

Angel Diaz had been convicted of burglary four times before he was 16. Diaz's lawyer, Paul Auerbach, said that Diaz was an honest boy forced by poverty to do bad things. Diaz was sentenced to 38 1/3 years to life on 13 counts of murder, robbery, burglary, and conspiracy. His accomplice, Victor Sanchez, 21, who worked for the murdered man and planned the murder, had already been sentenced to 15 years to life.[1]

As I write this chapter the National Center of Health Statistics has reported that the homicide rate for young men in the United States is 4 to 73 times the rate in other industrial countries. Whereas killings per

100,000 for men 15 through 24 years old in 1986 or 1987 were 0.3 in Austria and 0.5 in Japan, it was 21.9 in the United States and as high as 232 for blacks in some states. The nearest nation to the United States was Scotland, with a 5.0 homicide rate. In some central city areas it is 773 times the rate of that of men in Austria. The homicide rate in New York City broke the 2000 mark in 1990. Black males in Harlem are said to have a lower life expectancy than males in Bangladesh. Escalating crime has caused an erosion in the quality of urban living. It is threatening the fabric of our social life.

Homo sapiens is the only species in which it is common for an individual to kill another. In most species where there is a conflict between individuals, the weaker party submits to the stronger through some ritual gesture and is permitted to depart in peace. Only in captivity, where the defeated animal cannot get away, will it be killed. Human beings alone deliberately kill other individuals and groups of their own species. Perhaps it is not that we are more aggressive than other species but that our drives have been made more lethal by the use of weapons. A weapon allows us to harm or kill without actually making physical contact with our victim. A man with a gun need not even touch his victim. The inhibition against killing is undermined by the trigger's power, a point to be kept in mind when discussing gun control legislation. The airplane bomber need not even see his victims as he presses the button unleashing his destruction. We are a violent race whose power of destruction has increased in proportion to our technology.

Naturally, the subject of punishment should receive increased attention, as should the social causes of crime. As a radical student activist in the 60's, I once opposed increased police protection for my neighborhood in Morningside Heights, New York City, arguing that we must get to the causes of crime and not deal only with the symptoms. I later realized that this was like refusing fire fighters the use of water hoses to put out fires because they only dealt with the symptoms rather than causes of the fire.

The truth is that we do not know the exact nature of what causes crimes of violence. Many people in the United States believe that poverty causes crime, but this is false. Poverty is a terrible condition, but it is not a necessary or sufficient condition for violent crime. The majority of people in India are far poorer than most of the American poor, yet a person, male or female, can walk through the worst slum of Calcutta or New Delhi at any time of the day or night without fearing molestation. Drugs are another cause of crime, and the turn from heroin to crack as the "drug of choice" has exacerbated the matter, but plenty of crime occurred in our society before drug abuse became the problem it now is. We leave the subject of the causes of crime for psychologists and sociologists to solve and turn to the nature of punishment.

PUNISHMENT

To be responsible for a past act is to be liable to praise or blame. If the act was especially good, we go further than praise. We reward it. If it was especially evil, we go further than blame. We punish it. In this chapter let us examine the notions of punishment and capital punishment. First we need to inquire under what conditions, if any, criminal punishment is justified. We will look at three answers to this problem: the Retributivist, the Utilitarian, and the Rehabilitationist.

Even though few of us will ever become criminals nor be indicted on criminal charges, most of us feel very strongly about the matter of criminal punishment. Something about crime touches the deepest nerves of our imagination. Take the following situations, which are based on newspaper reports of the past few years.

1. A drug addict stabs to death a vibrant, gifted 22-year-old graduate student who has dedicated her life to helping others.
2. A sex-pervert lures little children into his home, sexually abuses them, and then kills them. Over 20 bodies are discovered on his property.
3. A man sends his wife and daughter on an airplane trip, puts a time bomb into their luggage, and takes out a million dollar insurance policy on them. The money will be used to pay off his gambling debts and for prostitutes.

What is it within us that rises up in indignation at the thought of these atrocities? What should happen to the criminals in these cases? How can the victims (or their loved ones) ever be compensated for these crimes? We feel conflicting emotional judgments of harsh vengeance toward the criminal and, at the same time, concern that we don't ourselves become violent and irrational in our quest for revenge.

The Definition of Punishment

We may define "punishment" as *a harm inflicted by a person in a position of authority upon another person who is judged to have violated a rule.*[2] It can be analyzed into five concepts:

1. *An Evil.* To punish is to inflict an unpleasantness or suffering (not necessarily pain). Regarding this concept, the question is: Under what conditions is it right to cause harm or inflict suffering?
2. *For an Offense.* Moral or legal? Should we punish everyone who commits a moral offense? Need the offense already have been committed?

3. *Done to the Offender.* At least the offender must be judged or believed to be guilty of a crime. Does this rule out the possibility of punishing innocent people? What should we call the process of framing the innocent and "punishing" them?
4. *Carried Out by a Personal Agency.* Punishment is not the work of natural consequences. Nature cannot punish. Only humans or conscious beings can do so.
5. *Imposed by an Authority.* Punishment is conferred through the institutions that maintain laws or the social code. This rules out vigilante executions as punishment.

Theories of Punishment

Retributivist Theories. Retributivist theories make infliction of punishment depend on what the agent deserves as one who has done wrong rather than on any future social utility that might result from the infliction of suffering on the criminal. That is, rather than focusing on any *future* good that might result from punishment, retributivist theories are *backward* looking, assessing the nature of the misdeed. The most forceful proponents of this view are Immanuel Kant (1724–1804) and C. S. Lewis (1898–1963). Their position has three theses.

1. Guilt is a necessary condition for justified punishment. That is, *only* the guilty may be punished.
2. Guilt is a sufficient condition for justified punishment. That is, *all* the guilty must be punished. If you have committed a crime, morality demands that you suffer for it.
3. The proper amount of punishment to be inflicted upon the morally (or legally) guilty offender is that amount which fits (is appropriate to) the moral gravity of the offense.

Punishment restores the scales of justice, the social equilibrium of benefits and burdens, and it is backward looking. We might put the argument this way.

1. In breaking a primary rule of society, a person obtains an unfair advantage over others.
2. Unfair advantages ought to be redressed by society if possible.
3. Punishment is a form of redressing the unfair advantage.
4. Therefore, we ought to punish the offender for breaking the primary rule. Punishment restores the social equilibrium of burdens and benefits by taking from the agent what he or she unfairly got and now owes—that is, exacting his or her debt.

Mitigating circumstances may be taken into consideration to lessen the severity of the punishment, but the aim is to bring about moral homeostasis, a social order in which the good are rewarded and the bad are punished in proportion to their deeds.

Although the retributivist theory has broad intuitive appeal, it is beset with problems. One problem is to make sense out of the notion of balancing the scales of justice. The metaphor suggests a cosmic scale that is put out of balance by a crime, but such a scale might not exist or if one does, it may not be our duty to maintain it through punishment. That may be God's role. Furthermore, retributivism seems unduly retrospective. If we can restore the repentant criminal to moral integrity through rehabilitative processes, then to insist on a pound of flesh seems barbaric. While retributivists usually moderate their stance in the light of these objections, the question is whether a sufficiently qualified retributivism is really a retributivism at all rather than a version of utilitarianism.

Utilitarian Theories.   Utilitarian theories are theories of deterrence, reform, and prevention. The emphasis is not on the gravity of the evil done but on deterring and preventing future evil. Their motto might be "Don't cry over spilt milk!" Unlike retributivist theories, which are backward looking and based on *desert*, utilitarian theories are *forward* looking, based on social improvement, the prevention and deterrence of future crimes. Jeremy Bentham (1748–1832) and John Stuart Mill (1806–1873) are classic utilitarians. Their position can be analyzed into three theses:

1. Social utility (correction, prevention, and deterrence) is a necessary condition for justified punishment.
2. Social utility is a sufficient condition for justified punishment.
3. The proper amount of punishment to be inflicted upon the offender is that amount which will do the most good (or least harm) to all those who will be affected by it. Anthony Benn puts it well: "The margin of increment of harm inflicted on the offender should be preferable to the harm avoided by fixing that penalty rather than one slightly lower."[3]

Punishment is a technique of social control, justified as long as it prevents more evil than it produces. If there exists a system of social control that will give a greater balance (for example, rehabilitation), then the utilitarian will opt for that. The utilitarian doesn't accept draconian laws that would deter because the punishment would be worse than the crime, causing greater suffering than the original offense. Only three grounds are permissible for punishment: (1) to prevent a repetition; (2) to deter others—the threat of punishment deters potential offenders; and (3) to rehabilitate the criminal (this need not be seen as punishment, but it may involve that).

The threat of punishment is everything. Every act of punishment is to that extent an admission of the failure of the threat. If the threat were successful, no punishment would be needed to be justified.

The weakness of utilitarianism is that it seems to allow the punishment of the innocent if that will deter others from crime. We want only criminals punished, but utilitarians focus on results, not justice. If we can frame an innocent bum for a rape and murder to prevent a riot, the utilitarian will be tempted to do so. This violates the essence of justice.

Rehabilitative Theories.   Crime is a disease, and the criminal is a sick person who needs to be cured, not punished. Rehabilitationists such as B. F. Skinner, Karl Menninger, and Benjamin Karpman point to the failure and cruelties of our penal system and advocate an alternative of therapy and reconditioning. "Therapy, not torture" might be said to be their motto. Criminals are not really in control of their behavior but are suffering personality disorders. Crime is by and large a result of an adverse early environment, so that what must be done is to recondition the criminal through positive reinforcement. Punishment is a prescientific response to antisocial behavior. At best punishment temporarily suppresses adverse behavior, but if untreated, Skinner argues, it will resurface again as if the punishment never occurred. It is useless as a deterrent. Rehabilitationists charge that retributivists are guilty of holding an antiquated notion of human beings as possessing free wills and being responsible for their behavior. We, including all of our behavior, are all products of our heredity and, especially, our environment.

Of course we need to confine criminals for their own good and society's, but a process of positive reinforcement must be the means of dealing with criminals and their "crimes." Benjamin Karpman, one of the proponents of this theory, puts it this way[4]:

> Basically, criminality is but a symptom of insanity, using the term in its widest generic sense to express unacceptable social behavior based on unconscious motivation flowing from a disturbed instinctive and emotional life, whether this appears in frank psychoses, or in less obvious form in neuroses and unrecognized psychoses. . . . If criminals are products of early environmental influences in the same sense that psychotics and neurotics are, then it should be possible to reach them psychotherapeutically.

Rehabilitation theories are challenged from many quarters. First, they seem to undermine the very notion of human autonomy and responsibility. Individuals who are not mentally ill are free agents whose actions should be taken seriously as flowing from free decisions. If a person kills in cold blood, he or she must bear the responsibility for that murder. Rehabilitation theories reduce moral problems to medical problems.

Furthermore, rehabilitation doesn't seem to work. Rehabilitation is a form of socialization through sophisticated medical treatment. While humans are malleable, socialization and medical technology have limits. Socialization can be relatively effective in infancy and early childhood, less so in late childhood, and even less so in adulthood. Perhaps at some future time when brain manipulation becomes possible, we will make greater strides toward behavior modification. The question then will be whether we have a right to tamper with someone's psyche in this manner. And won't that tampering itself be a form of punishment?

John Rawls in a classic paper, "Two Concepts of Rules," attempts to do justice to both the retributivist and the utilitarian theories of punishment.[5] Rawls argues that there is a difference between justifying an institution and justifying a given instance where the institution is applied. The question, "Why do we have law or system?" is of a different nature from the question, "Why are we applying the law in the present situation in this mode?" Applied to punishment: (1) "Why do we have a system of punishment?" and (2) "Why are we harming John for his misdeed?" are two different sorts of question. When we justify the institution of punishment we resort to utilitarian considerations: A society in which the wicked prosper will offer inadequate inducement to virtue. The society will get on better if some rules are made and enforced than a society in which no rules exist or they are not enforced. But when we seek to justify an individual application of punishment, we resort to retributivist considerations, for example. We reason that if someone comitted a breach against the law, he or she merits a fitting punishment.

CAPITAL PUNISHMENT

The death penalty has been used widely throughout history for just about every crime imaginable. In the seventh century B.C. Draco's Athenian code prescribed the death penalty for stealing fruit. Later Athenians were executed for making misleading public speeches. The criminal code of the Holy Roman Empire and later Europe punished sorcery, arson, blasphemy, sodomy, and counterfeiting by burning at the stake.

Most of us are appalled by this indiscriminate use of the death penalty, and many abolitionists—those who oppose capital punishment—argue that all uses of the death penalty are barbaric, "cruel and unusual" punishments, which only degrade humankind.

Proponents of capital punishment justify it either from a retributive or a utilitarian framework, and you could use both theories for a combined justification. Abolitionists deny that these arguments for capital punishment are valid, because the sanctity of human life, which gives each person a right to life, is inconsistent with the practice of putting criminals to death.

The retributivist argues that (1) *all* the guilty deserve to be punished; (2) *only* the guilty deserve to be punished; and (3) the guilty deserve a punishment equal in severity to their crime. It follows that all those who commit capital offenses deserve capital punishments.

A classic expression of the retributivist position on capital punishment is Kant's statement that if an offender "has committed murder, he must *die*. In this case, no possible substitute can satisfy justice. For there is no *parallel* between death and even the most miserable life, so that there is no equality of crime and retribution unless the perpetrator is judicially put to death (at all events without any maltreatment which might make humanity an object of horror in the person of the sufferer)." Kant illustrates his doctrine of exact retribution[6]:

> Even if a civil society were to dissolve itself with the consent of all its members (for example, if a people who inhabited an island decided to separate and disperse to other parts of the world), the last murderer in prison would first have to be executed in order that each should receive his just deserts and that the people should not bear the guilt of a capital crime through failing to insist on its punishment; for if they do not do so, they can be regarded as accomplices in the public violation of justice.

For Kant the death penalty was a conclusion of the argument for justice: just recompense to the victim and just punishment to the offender. As a person of dignity the victim deserves to have the offender harmed in proportion to the gravity of the crime, and as a person of high worth and responsibility, the offender shows himself or herself deserving of capital punishment.

Let us expand on the retributivist argument. Each person has a right to life. But criminal C violates an innocent person V's right to life by threatening it or by killing V. The threat to V constitutes a grave offense, but taking V's life constitutes a capital offense. Attempting to take V's life, from a moral point of view, is equivalent to taking the life. C deserves to be put to death for the offense.

But the abolitionist responds, "No, putting C to death only compounds evil. If killing is an evil, then the state actually doubles the evil by executing the murderer. The state violates C's right to life."

But the abolitionist is mistaken on two counts. First, the state does not violate C's right to life. C has already forfeited any right C had to life in murdering V. The right to life is not an absolute right that can never be overridden. It is a serious *prima facie* right that can be jettisoned only by a more weighty moral reason. In this case the violating of V's right is sufficient reason for overriding C's right to life. Secondly, while killing C may be an evil, it is a lesser of evils, which may be justified. Not to right a wrong, not to punish the criminal, may be a worse evil than harming the criminal.

On the retributivist account, the criminal *forfeits* his or her right to life by deliberately murdering the victim. But forfeiture does not tell the whole story. Not only do murderers forfeit their lives, but they positively deserve their punishment. If they have committed a capital offense, they deserve a capital punishment. If first-degree murder is on the level of the worst type of crimes, as we think it is, then we are justified in imposing the worst type of punishments on the murderer. Death would be the fitting punishment; anything less would lessen the seriousness of the offense.

We do know of crimes worse than murder—torturing victims over a long period and driving them insane is worse than murdering them. Perhaps society should torture the torturers and the rapists (it would be too repulsive to rape them). The ancient Lex Talionis ("the law of the claw," "an eye for an eye, a tooth for a tooth, a life for a life," Exodus 22) practiced in ancient Israel might imply such practices. For most of us, death seems an adequate punishment for the worst types of crimes—though strictly speaking it may not be anywhere near to the proportion of suffering or evil done by the criminal. How could we punish Hitler in proportion to the gravity of his offense? There are limits to what punishment can and should do. Nothing more than death seems right. The question is whether something less than death would do as well, say, long-term prison sentences.

A moderate retributivist might allow mercy to enter the picture earlier. If society is secure, it might well opt to show mercy and not execute murderers. Utilitarian reasons may enter into the calculation. Retributivism may be mitigated by utilitarian considerations, not because the criminal doesn't deserve the death penalty, but because a secure society isn't threatened as a whole by occasional murders, heinous though they be. In a secure society (Scandinavian or Swiss societies come to mind, with crime rates a tiny fraction of that of the United States) capital offenses are not tearing away at the very fabric of the social order.

The utilitarian argument for capital punishment is that it deters would-be offenders from committing first-degree murder. The evidence for this is weak. We lack evidence that capital punishment deters, but this should not be construed as evidence for the lack of deterrence. There is no such evidence for nondeterrence. We simply don't know. Statistics are hard to read, though common sense gives credence to the hypothesis that the threat of the death penalty deters. Some of the evidence is anecdotal, as the following story shows. The British member of parliament Arthur Lewis was converted from abolitionism to supporting the death penalty. Here is an account of his change of mind.[7]

> One reason that has stuck in my mind, and which has proved to me beyond question, is that there was once a professional burglar in [my] constituency who consistently boasted of the fact that he had spent about one-third of his life in prison. . . . He said to me 'I am a professional burglar. Before we go out on a job we plan it down to every detail. Before we go into the boozer to have a drink we say "Don't forget, no shooters"—shooters being guns. He adds 'We did our job and didn't have shooters because at that time there was capital punishment. Our wives, girlfriends, and our mums said, "Whatever you do, do not carry a shooter because if you are caught you might be topped." If you do away with capital punishment they will all be carrying shooters.'

Being "topped" refers to being executed.

It is difficult to know how widespread this reasoning is. Perhaps it is mainly confined to a certain class of professional burglars or middle-class people who are tempted to kill their enemies. We simply don't know how much capital punishment deters or whether the deterrence is negligible.

John Stuart Mill admitted that capital punishment does not inspire terror in hardened criminals, but it may well make an impression on prospective murderers. "As for what is called the failure of the death punishment, who is able to judge of that? We partly know who those are whom it has not deterred; but who is there who knows whom it has deterred, or how many human beings it has saved who would have lived to be murderers if that awful association had not been thrown round the idea of murder from their earliest infancy."[8]

In this regard, Ernest van den Haag's Best Bet argument should be noted.[9] Van den Haag has argued that even though we don't know for certain whether the death penalty prevents other murders, we should bet that it does. Indeed, owing to our ignorance, any social policy we take is a gamble. Not to choose capital punishment for first-degree murder is as much a bet that capital punishment doesn't deter as choosing the policy is a bet that it does. There is a significant difference in the betting, however, in that to bet against capital punishment is to bet against the innocent, while to bet for it is to bet against the murderer and for the innocent.

Suppose that we choose a policy of capital punishment for capital crimes. In this case we are betting that the death of some murderers will be more than compensated by the lives of some innocents not being murdered (either by these murderers or others who would have murdered, for example, Lewis's burglar). If we're right, we have saved the lives of the innocent. If we're wrong, unfortunately, we've sacrificed the lives of some murderers. But say we choose not to have a social policy of capital punishment. If capital punishment doesn't work as a deterrent, we've come out ahead, but if it does, then we've missed an opportunity to save innocent lives. If we value the saving of innocent lives more highly than the loss of the guilty, then to bet on a policy of capital punishment turns out to be rational. The reasoning goes like this. Let "CP" stand for "capital punishment":

	CP Works	*CP Doesn't Work*
We bet on CP	a. We win: some murders die and some innocents are saved.	b. We lose: some murderers die for no purpose.
We bet against CP	c. We lose: murders live and some innocents needlessly die.	d. We win: murderers live and the lives of others are unaffected.

Suppose that we estimate that the utility value of a murderer's life is 5 while the value of an innocent's life is 10 (it's at least two times the value of the murderer's life). The sums work out this way:

A murderer saved	+5
A murderer executed	−5
An innocent saved	+10
An innocent murdered	−10

Suppose that for each execution only two innocent lives are spared. Then the outcomes read as follows:

a. −5 + 20 = +15
b. −5
c. +5 −20 = − 15
d. +5

If all the possibilities are roughly equal, we can sum their outcomes like this:

If we bet on capital punishment (a) and (b) obtain = +10.
If we bet against capital punishment (c) and (d) obtain = −10.
So to execute convicted murderers turns out to be a good bet. To abolish the death penalty for convicted murderers would be a bad bet. We unnecessarily put the innocent at risk.

Even if we value the utility of an innocent life only slightly more than that of the murderer's, it is still rational to execute convicted murderers. As van den Haag writes, "Though we have no proof of the positive deterrence of the penalty, we also have no proof of zero or negative effectiveness. I believe we have no right to risk additional future victims of murder for the sake of sparing convicted murderers; on the contrary, our moral obligation is to risk the possible ineffectiveness of executions."[10]

You may object that this kind of quantifying of human life is entirely inappropriate. But if you do make this objection, you should object to it in other places too (see Chapter 2 on the sanctity of life).

Objections to Capital Punishment

Let us examine the major objections to capital punishment as well as the retentionist's responses to those objections.

1. Objection: Capital punishment is a morally unacceptable thirst for revenge. As former British Prime Minister Edward Heath put it,[11]

> The real point which is emphasized to me by many constituents is that even if the death penalty is not a deterrent, murderers deserve to die. This is the question of revenge. Again, this will be a matter of moral judgment for each of us. I do not believe in revenge. If I were to become the victim of terrorists, I would not wish them to be hanged or killed in any other way for revenge. All that would do is deepen the bitterness which already tragically exists in the conflicts we experience in society, particularly in Northern Ireland.

Response: Retributivism is not to be equated with revenge, although their motifs are often intermixed in practice. Revenge is a personal response to a perpetrator for an injury. Retribution is an impartial and impersonal response to an offender for an offense done against someone. You cannot want revenge for the harm of someone to whom you are indifferent. Revenge always involves personal concern for the victim. Retribution is not personal but based on objective factors: the criminal has deliberately harmed an innocent party and so *deserves* to be punished, whether I wish it or not. I would agree that I or my son or daughter *deserves* to be punished for our crimes, but I don't wish any vengeance on myself or my son or daughter.

Furthermore, while revenge often leads us to exact more suffering from the offender than the offense warrants, retribution stipulates that the offender be punished in proportion to the gravity of the offense. In this sense, the *lex talionis* that we find in the Old Testament is actually a progressive rule, where retribution replaces revenge as the mode of punishment. It says that there are limits to what one can do to the offender. Revenge demands a life for an eye or a tooth, but Moses gives a rule that exacts a penalty equal to the harm done by the offender.

2. Objection: Capital punishment is to be rejected because of human fallibility in convicting innocent parties and sentencing them to death. While some compensation is available to those unjustly imprisoned, the death sentence is irrevocable. We can't compensate the dead. As John Maxton, a member of the British Parliament, puts it, "If we allow one innocent person to be executed, morally we are committing the same or, in some ways, a worse crime than the person who committed the murder."[12]

Response: Mr. Maxton is incorrect in saying that mistaken judicial execution is morally the same as or worse than murder, for a deliberate intention to kill the innocent occurs in a murder, whereas in wrongful capital punishment no such intention occurs.

Sometimes this objection is framed this way: better that we let 10 criminals go free than execute one innocent person. If this dictum is a call for safeguards, then it is well taken, but somewhere there seems to be a limit on the tolerance of society toward capital offenses. Would these abolitionists argue that it is better that 50 or 100 or 1000 murderers go free than that one innocent person be executed? Society has a right to protect itself from capital offenses even if this means taking a finite chance of mistakenly executing an innocent person.

That we can err in applying the death penalty should give us pause and cause us to build an appeals process into the judicial system. Such a process is already present in the American and British legal systems. That an occasional error may be made, regrettable though this is, is not a sufficient reason for us to refuse to use the death penalty, if on balance it serves a just and useful function.

3. Objection: The death penalty constitutes a denial of the wrongdoer's essential dignity as a human being. No matter how bad a person becomes, no matter how terrible one's deed, we must never cease to regard a person as an end in himself or herself, as someone with inherent dignity. Capital punishment violates that dignity. As Thurgood Marshall stated in *Gregg v. Georgia* (quoted at the beginning of this chapter), the death penalty "has as its very basis the total denial of the wrongdoer's dignity and worth . . . [and] is an excessive penalty forbidden by the Eighth and Fourteen Amendments."

Margaret Falls argues eloquently that treating people as moral agents prohibits us from executing them. "Holding an offender responsible necessarily includes demanding that she respond as only moral agents can: by reevaluating her behavior. If the punishment meted out makes reflective response to it impossible, then it is not a demand for response as a moral agent. Death is not a punishment to which reflective moral response is possible. . . . Death terminates the possibility of moral reform."[13]

Response: Rather than being a violation of the wrongdoer's dignity, capital punishment may constitute a recognition of human dignity. As we noted in discussing Kant's view of retribution, the use of capital punishment respects the worth of the victim in calling for an equal punishment to be exacted from the offender, and it respects the dignity of the offender in treating him or her as a free agent who must be respected for his or her decisions and who must bear as a responsible agent the cost of his or her acts .

First it respects the worth of the victim. The columnist Mike Royko bluntly put it this way[14]:

> When I think of the thousands of inhabitants of Death Rows in the hundreds of prisons in this country, I don't react the way the kindly souls do—with revulsion that the state would take these lives. My reaction is: What's taking us so long? Let's get that electrical current flowing. Drop the pellets now!
>
> Whenever I argue this with friends who have opposite views, they say that I don't have enough regard for that most marvelous of miracles—human life.
>
> Just the opposite: It's because I have so much regard for human life that I favor capital punishment. Murder is the most terrible crime there is. Anything less than the death penalty is an insult to the victim and society. It says, in effect, that we don't value the victim's life enough to punish the killer fully.

It is just because the *victim's* life is sacred that the death penalty is a fitting punishment for first-degree murder.

Secondly, it's precisely because murderers are autonomous, free agents, that we regard their acts of murder as their own and hold them responsible. Not to hold them responsible for their crimes is to treat them as less than autonomous. Just as we praise and reward people in proportion to the merit of their good deeds, so we blame and punish them in proportion to the evil of their bad deeds. If there is evidence that the offender did not act freely, we would mitigate his sentence. But if the offender did act of his or her own free will, he or she bears the responsibility for those actions and deserves to be punished accordingly.

To Meg Falls's argument that the death penalty makes moral reform impossible, two things must be said. (1) It's false, and (2) it's not an argument for the complete abolition of capital punishment.

1. **It's false.** The criminal may be given time to repent of his or her offense before execution. It is hard to know when the murderer has truly repented and has been rehabilitated, since faking it is in the murderer's self-interest, but even if he or she does repent, the heinousness of the deed remains and the murderer should receive his or her just desert.

2. Even if some offenders were suitably rehabilitated, and even if we had a policy of showing mercy to those who gave strong evidence of having been morally reformed, many criminals may well be incurable, given our present means for rehabilitation and moral reform. Present rehabilitation programs are not very successful.

Of course, there are counterresponses to all the retentionist's responses. Consider the utilitarian matter of cost. The appeals process, which is necessary to our system of justice, is so prolonged and costly that it might not be worth the costs simply to satisfy our sense of retribution. Furthermore, most moderate retributivists do not argue that there is an *absolute* duty to execute first-degree murderers. Even the principle that the guilty should suffer in proportion to the harm they caused is not absolute. It can be overridden by mercy. But such mercy must be judicious, serving the public good.

In the same vein many argue that life imprisonment without parole will accomplish just as much as the death penalty. The retentionist would respond that death is a more fitting punishment for one who kills in cold blood, and deterrentists would be concerned about the possibility of escape and the enormous costs of keeping a prisoner encarcerated for life. But imprisonment without parole is an alternative to the death penalty that should be given serious consideration.

No doubt we should work toward the day when capital punishment is no longer necessary, when the murder rate becomes a tiny fraction of what it is today, when a civilized society can safely incarcerate the few violent criminals in its midst, and where moral reform of the criminal is a reality. Both the abolitionist and the retentionist can agree on that.

Study Questions

1. Discuss the three major theories of punishment. Which one seems most persuasive? How does each bear on the question of capital punishment?

2. Is retributivism essentially revenge? Is it an emotion unfitting for rational and moral creatures?

3. Some have claimed that in executing criminals the state simply carries on the horrid tradition of murder. Do you agree? Is capital punishment simply judicial murder? Or does retributivism simply mirror our notion of distributive justice? That is, if we should receive awards or wages according to our merits, shouldn't we also receive punishment according to our demerits?

4. Compare your views on the sanctity of life/quality of life question to your views on capital punishment. Do you see any relationship?

5. Is Thurgood Marshall correct in arguing that the death penalty is "cruel and unusual punishment," a violation of the Eighth Amendment?

6. Do you think that the death penalty deters murder? Would it deter any crime? Explain your answer.

7. Discuss Ernest van den Haag's Best Bet argument. Is it a sound argument?

8. Some have argued that life imprisonment without parole is an adequate punishment for a cold-blooded murder, so that we don't need the death penalty. Do you agree? Discuss the pros and cons of this position.

Endnotes

1. "Jail for Crime that Shocked Even the Jaded," *The New York Times*, August 16, 1990.

2. In the following analysis I am indebted to Anthony Flew, "Justification of Punishment," *Philosophy* (1954) and Herbert Morris, "Persons and Punishment," *The Monist* 52 (October 1968).

3. Stanley Benn, "Punishment," in Paul Edwards, ed., *Encyclopedia of Philosophy*, (New York: Macmillan Inc., 1967), vol. 7, pp. 29–35.

4. Benjamin Karpman, "Criminal Psychodynamics," *Journal of Criminal Law and Criminology* 47 (1956), p. 9. See also B. F. Skinner, *Science and Human Behavior* (New York: Macmillan, 1953), especially pages 182–193, and Karl Menninger, *The Crime of Punishment* (New York: Viking, 1968).

5. John Rawls, "Two Concepts of Rules," *Philosophical Review* (1955).

6. Immanuel Kant, *The Metaphysics of Morals*, John Ladd, trans. (Indianapolis: Bobbs-Merrill, 1965), p. 103.

7. British *Parliamentary Debates*, fifth series, vol. 23, issue 1243, House of Commons, May 11, 1982. Quoted in Tom Sorell, *Moral Theory and Capital Punishment* (Oxford: Blackwell, 1987), p. 36.

8.. *Parliamentary Debates*, third series, April 21, 1868. Reprinted in Peter Singer, ed., *Applied Ethics* (Oxford: Oxford University Press, 1986), pp. 97–104.

9. Ernst van den Haag, "On Deterrence and the Death Penalty," *Ethics* 78 (July 1968), pp. 107–115.

10. Ibid, p. 114.

11. British *Parliamentary Debates*, 1982, quoted in Sorell, op. cit., p. 43.

12. Ibid, p. 47.

13. Margaret Falls, "Against the Death Penalty: A Christian Stance in a Secular World," *Christian Century* (December 10, 1986), pp. 1118, 1119.

14. Mike Royko, *Chicago Sun-Times*, September 1983.

CHAPTER 8

Animal Rights

Brute beasts, not having understanding and therefore not being persons, cannot have any rights. . . . The conclusion is clear. We have no duties to them,—not of justice, . . . not of religion . . .

—JOSEPH RICKABY, S.J., MORAL PHILOSOPHY OF ETHICS AND NATURAL LAW (1889).

In their behavior towards creatures, all men are Nazis.

—ISAAC BASHEVIS SINGER, *ENEMIES: A LOVE STORY*

INTRODUCTION: ALL IS NOT WELL IN THE ANIMAL KINGDOM

On average, 100 animals are killed in laboratories in the United States every minute. Fifty million experimental animals are put to death each year.[1] Some die in the testing of industrial and cosmetic products, some are disposed of because they are female, some are killed after being forced fed or after being tested with pharmaceutical drugs. Insecticides, pesticides, antifreeze chemicals, brake fluids, bleaches, Christmas tree sprays, silver cleaners, oven cleaners, deodorants, skin fresheners, baby preparations, bubble bath soap, bath salts, freckle creams, eye make-up, crayons, fire extinguishers, inks, suntan oils, nail polish, mascara, hair sprays, zipper lubricants, paints—all are tested on animals before humans are allowed to use them. Although not required in all cases, many companies have traditionally performed animal tests to gain approval of their products by the government. Legal requirements that animals be anesthetized can be circumvented in many experiments, and in others the nature of the tests preclude the use of anesthesia. In the Draize eye test concentrated solutions of commercial products are instilled into rabbits' eyes and the damage is then recorded according to the size of the

103

area injured. Monkeys have been used for these experiments. After the tests, the animals are destroyed.[2]

Civet cats are confined in small cages in dark rooms where the temperature is 110°F, until they die. The musk, which is scraped from their genitals once a day for as long as they can survive, makes the scent of perfume last a bit longer after each application. In recent years progress has been made in that several cosmetic companies are abandoning the use of animals for testing in cosmetic products.

In military primate equilibrium studies, monkeys are set in simulated flying platforms and tested for their ability to keep their balance under duress. They are subjected to high doses of radiation and chemical warfare agents to see how these would affect their ability to fly. When they become nauseated and begin to vomit from the doses of radiation, they are forced to keep their platform horizontal through the inducement of electric shocks.

In July 1973 Representative Les Aspin of Wisconsin discovered that the United States Air Force was planning to purchase 200 beagle puppies with vocal cords tied to prevent normal barking to be used for testing poisonous gases. At the same time the Army was preparing to use 400 beagles for similar tests. More recently Army laboratories fed 60 beagles with doses of TNT to determine the effects of the explosive on animals.[3]

At several universities dogs, monkeys, and rats have been confined to small rooms where they are unable to escape from electric shocks emanating from the steel grid floors in order to determine how they will react to unavoidable pain. In toxicity tests animals are placed in sealed chambers and forced to inhale sprays, gases, and vapors. In dermal toxicity tests rabbits have their fur removed so that a test substance can be placed on their skin. The skin may bleed, blister, and peel. In immersion studies animals are placed in vats of diluted substances, sometimes causing them to drown before the results can be obtained.

Rhesus monkeys have been given massive doses of cocaine until they began to mutilate themselves and eventually die of cocaine abuse. In 1984 at a major university, experiments were performed on baboons to determine brain damage from head injuries. The subjects were strapped down in boxlike vices and had specially designed helmets glued to their skulls. Then a pneumatic device delivered calibrated blows to the helmet, causing brain injuries to the baboons. Videotapes showed that while the head injuries were being inflicted the researchers stood by joking about their subjects.[4]

Neither is all well down at McDonald's "factory farm." High-tech machinery has replaced the bucolic pleasantries of free range agriculture. Old farmer McDonald doesn't visit his hens in barns to pick an egg from the comfortable nest. Now as soon as the chicks are hatched they are placed in small cages. Between five and eight (up to nine) chickens are pressed close together in cages about 18 inches by 10 inches over thin wired floors which hurt their feet and where they cannot move around. They are painfully debeaked so that they cannot attack each other in these unnatural quarters. In other chicken factories the chicken are hung by their feet from a conveyer belt that escorts them through an automatic throat slicing machine. Three billion chickens are killed in the United States each year. Likewise, pigs and veal calves are kept in pens so small that they cannot move or turn around and develop muscles. They are separated from their mothers so they cannot be suckled and are fed a diet low in iron so that we can eat very tender meat.[5] James Rachels describes the process this way[6]:

> Veal calves spend their lives in pens too small to allow them to turn around or even to lie down comfortably—exercise toughens the muscles, which reduces the "quality" of the meat, and besides, allowing the animals adequate living space would be prohibitively expensive. In these pens the calves cannot perform such basic actions as grooming themselves, which they naturally desire to do, because there in not room for them to twist their heads around. It is clear that the calves miss their mothers, and like human infants they want something to suck: they can be seen trying vainly to suck the sides of their stalls. In order to keep their meat pale and tasty, they are fed a liquid diet deficient in both iron and roughage. Naturally they develop cravings for these things, because they need them. The calf's craving for iron is so strong that, if it is allowed to turn around, it will lick at its own urine, although calves normally find this repugnant. The tiny stall, which prevents the animal from turning, solves this "problem." The craving for roughage is especially strong for bedding, since the animal would be driven to eat it, and that would spoil the meat. For these animals the slaughterhouse is not an unpleasant end to an otherwise contented life. As terrifying as the process of slaughter is, for them it may actually be regarded as a merciful release.

FIVE THEORIES OF OBLIGATION TO ANIMALS

Five theories on the moral status of animals appear in the history of Western philosophy and religion, from assigning animals no status on the one extreme to assigning them equal status with humans on the other extreme.

1. The No Status Theory

The No Status theory was set forth by René Descartes (1596–1650), who held that animals have no rights or moral status because they have no

souls. Since, according to Descartes, the soul is necessary to consciousness, animals cannot feel pain or pleasure. They are mere machines.
"From this aspect the body is regarded as a machine which, having been
made by the hands of God, is incomparably better arranged, and
possesses in itself movements which are much more admirable than any
of those which can be invented by man." [7]

According to Descartes, animals are automata who move and bark
and utter sounds like well-wound clocks. Because they lack a soul, which
is the locus of consciousness and value, they have no moral status
whatsoever. It is no more morally wrong to pull the ears off a dog or eat
a cow than it is to kick a stone or eat a carrot.

We now know that Descartes was wrong. Animals do feel pain and
pleasure. They have consciousness and engage in purposeful behavior.
Dogs and cats manifest intelligence, gorillas and chimpanzees exhibit
complex abstracting and reasoning abilities and have the capacity to
communicate through language. The differences between humans and
other animals are more a matter of degree than of kind.

The nineteenth-century British philosopher William Whewell seems
to have held a slightly different version of the No Status view. "The
pleasures of animals are elements of a very different order from the
pleasures of man. We are bound to endeavor to augment the pleasures
of men, not only because they are pleasures, but because they are human
pleasures. We are bound to men by the universal tie of humanity, of
human brotherhood. We have no such tie to animals." [8]

This modified Cartesian view is reflected in Nobel Prize–winning
microbiologist David Baltimore's claim that no moral issue is involved in
animal research and in the writings of psychologists G. Gallup and S. D.
Suarez, who write that "the evolution of moral and ethical behavior in
man may be such that it is not applicable to other species." [9] Similarly, the
veterinarian F. S. Jacobs writes that "domestic animals exist in this world
because they fulfill man's needs. . . . Therefore it is meaningless to speak
of their rights to existence, because they would not exist if man did not
exist." [10]

2. The Indirect Obligation Theory

The dominant position in Western philosophy and religion has been the
view that while animals have no rights in their own right, we ought to treat
them kindly. We have duties to them because we have obligations to
rational beings, God, and other people who own them.

The creation story of Genesis supports a stewardship model of
creation. All of nature has been given to human beings for their use, but
humanity must use it properly for God's sake. "And God blessed [man
and woman] and God said to them, 'Be fruitful and multiply, and fill the

earth and subdue it; and have dominion over the fish of the sea and over the birds of the air and over every living thing that moves upon the earth.' And God said, 'Behold, I have given you every plant yielding seed which is upon the face of all the earth, and every tree with seed in its fruit; you shall have them for food.'"

Thomas Aquinas (1225–1274) and Immanuel Kant (1724–1804) hold that cruelty to animals is wrong because it forms bad character and leads to cruelty to human beings. Aquinas holds to an hierarchical view that permits humans to use animals for human good.[11]

> There is no sin in using a thing for the purpose for which it is. Now the order of things is such that the imperfect are for the perfect . . . thing, like plants which merely have life, are all alike for animals, and all animals are for man. Wherefore it is not unlawful if men use plants for the good of animals, and animals for the good of man, as the Philosopher [Aristotle] states.
>
> Now the most necessary use would seem to consist in the fact that animals use plants, and men use animals, for food, and this cannot be done unless these be deprived of life, wherefore it is lawful both to take life from plants for the use of animals and animals for the use of men. In fact this is in keeping with the commandment of God himself (Genesis 1:29, 30 and Genesis 9:3)

Aquinas goes on to say that we do have indirect obligations to animals, for the way we treat them will doubtless spill over into the way we treat fellow humans. "If any passages of Holy Writ seem to forbid us to be cruel to dumb animals, for instance to kill a bird with its young: this is either to remove man's thoughts from being cruel to other men, and lest through being cruel to animals one become cruel to human beings: or because injury to an animal leads to the temporal hurt of man, either of the doer of the deed, or of another."[12]

Kant repeats Aquinas's view. We have "no direct duties" to animals, for they "are not self-conscious and are there merely as a means to an end."[13]

> The end is man. . . . Our duties towards animals are merely indirect duties towards humanity. Animal nature has analogies to human nature, and by doing our duties to animals in respect to manifestations of human nature, we indirectly do our duty to humanity. . . . If a man shoots his dog because the animal is no longer capable of service, he does not fail in his duty to the dog, for the dog cannot judge, but his act is inhuman and damages in itself that humanity which it is his duty to show towards mankind. If he is not to stifle his human feelings, he must practice kindness towards animals, for he who is cruel to animals becomes hard also in his dealing with men.

The weakness of the Indirect Obligation view is that it makes rational self-consciousness the sole criterion for being morally considerable. While such self-consciousness may be the criterion for having full-blooded rights and for being a morally responsible agent, it is not the only thing of moral importance. Causing pain and suffering are bad in themselves, and we have duties not to do such but rather to ameliorate and eliminate pain and suffering.

3. The Equal Status View

The codirector of the animal rights group People for the Ethical Treatment of Animals (PETA) has said, "There is no rational basis for separating out the human animal. A rat is a pig is a dog is a boy. They're all mammals. . . . In time, we'll look on those who work in [animal laboratories] with the horror now reserved for the men and women who experimented on Jews in Auschwitz. . . . That, too, the Nazis said, was 'for the greater benefit of the master race.'"[14]

We call the view that equates human beings with animals the Equal Status thesis. Its foremost proponent is the philosopher Tom Regan who seeks to achieve three goals related to the treatment of animals: (1) The total abolition of the use of animals in science; (2) the total dissolution of commercial animal agriculture; and (3) the total elimination of commercial and sport hunting and trapping. Even though Regan concedes that some individual uses of animals for biomedical experimentation might be justified and free-range grazing farming is better than factory farming, all these uses constitute infringements on animal rights, and the exceptional cases are so isolated as to serve only to confuse the issue.

According to Regan, what is wrong is not the pain caused, the suffering, or the deprivation, though these compound the wrong. What's fundamentally wrong is "the system that allows us to view animals as *our resources*, here for us—to be eaten, or surgically manipulated, or put in our cross hairs for sport or money."[15]

Why is it wrong to treat animals as our resources? Because they have *inherent value* and are ends in themselves just like ourselves. They are of *equal worth* to human beings.[16]

> To say we have such value is to say that we are something more than, something different from, mere receptacles. Moreover, to insure that we do not pave the way for such injustices as slavery or sexual discrimination, we must believe that all who have inherent value have it equally, regardless of their sex, race, religion, birthplace, and so on. Similarly to be discarded as irrelevant are one's talents or skills, intelligence and wealth, personality or pathology, whether

one is loved or admired—or despised and loathed. The genius and the retarded child, the prince and the pauper, the brain surgeon and the fruit vendor, Mother Theresa and the most unscrupulous used car salesman—all have inherent value, all possess it equally, and all have an equal right to be treated with respect, to be treated in ways that do not reduce them to the status of things, as if they exist as resources for others.

What is the basis of the equal inherent value? Just this: " We are each of us the experiencing subject of a life, each of us a conscious creature having an individual welfare that has importance to us whatever our usefulness to others. We want and prefer things; believe and feel things; recall and expect things."

Several problems arise in Regan's theory of equal inherent value. First, he hasn't explained why being an experiencing subject grants one inherent value. If it does grant one a value, it seems a minimal value, one that is exceeded by the value of being *self-conscious*, especially rationally self-conscious. Someone in a daze or dream may be minimally conscious, but that is a state less valuable than being fully self-conscious with plans and projects. It is desirable to have more reason or intelligence rather than less reason or intelligence. Intelligence, knowledge, and freedom are inherent values, but animals have less of them than humans. It's true that humans have varying degrees of them, but as a species we have more of what makes for worth than other species, so that we must feel dissatisfied with Regan's assessment. He simply has not given any evidence for the thesis that all animals have equal worth and are to be treated with equal respect.

Regan rejects the notion of differing degrees of inherent value based on differing degrees of self-awareness or some other mental capability, affirming that this leads to the view that mentally superior people have stronger moral rights than mentally inferior people.

Recalling our discussion of the principle of the quality of life (Chapter 2), we have at least two ways to respond to Regan here. First, following deontologists like Kant and Rawls, we may appeal to the threshold view of self-consciousness and argue that all and only those who are capable of rational deliberation and life plans are to be accorded a serious right to life. While humans may differ with regard to their ability to reason, almost all (excepting the seriously retarded or insane) have sufficient ability to be counted within the circle of full moral citizenry. Some higher animals, such as dolphins, apes, and chimpanzees, may also belong to this group.

The second way to respond to Regan's anti-hierarchical notion of value is to concede with contractualists that no such thing as inherent value exists, but that animals simply are not part of the social contract.

Since rights derive from contract, animals do not have any rights. Of course, the contractualist may still recommend kindness to creatures outside of the contract, but where human interests are urgent, animals may be sacrificed to those interests.

What underlies Regan's view is the Sanctity of Life principle we examined in Chapter 2 of this book. He has imported a quasireligious view unsupported by sound argument or evidence. Essentially Regan's position reduces to the Sanctity of Life principle, which was shown to be very weak. Apart from an implicit appeal to the Sanctity of Life principle, Regan has given us no reason to accept any of his absolutist goals: the total abolition of the use of animals in scientific experimentation; the total dissolution of commercial animal agriculture; and the total elimination of commercial and sport hunting and trapping. So, following Regan, if we do not accept the Sanctity of Life principle, we will not be persuaded to adhere to any of these aims. Since many of us do not accept the Sanctity of Life principle, we still do not have good reasons to follow his proposals.

4. The Equal Consideration Theory

The Equal Consideration Theory was first set forth by Jeremy Bentham (1748–1832), the father of classic utilitarianism, and developed by Peter Singer in his epoch-making book *Animal Liberation* (1975). It is less radical than Regan's Equal Status theory but still accords animals serious moral consideration. Animals are just like us in basic morally relevant ways. As a utilitarian Bentham believed that the essence of morality was to promote happiness and the elimination of suffering. Animals are capable of happiness and suffering, so they are morally considerable in the same way that human beings are. In a classic passage Bentham compares the irrationality of our views toward animals with the irrationality of our views toward other races.[17]

> The day *may come*, when the rest of the animal creation may acquire those rights which never could have been withholden from them but by the hand of tyranny. The French have already discovered that the blackness of the skin is no reason why a human being should be abandoned without redress to the caprice of a tormentor. It may come one day to be recognized, that the number of the legs [or] the villosity of the skin are reasons equally insufficient for abandoning a sensitive being to the same fate. What else is it that should trace the insuperable line? Is it the faculty of reason, or, perhaps, the faculty of discourse? But a full-grown horse or dog is beyond comparison a more rational, as well as a more conversable animal, than an infant of a day, or a week, or even a month, old. But suppose the case were otherwise, what would it avail? The question is not, Can they *reason?* nor Can they *talk?* but, Can they *suffer?*

The main weakness of Bentham's account is that like Regan's view it equates humans and animals, so that if a chicken and a child are suffering equal pain, and we only have one pain reliever, we have a genuine moral dilemma on our hands. We might consider giving it to the chicken.

A related weakness of Bentham's view is that it reduces all morality to considerations of pleasure and pain. If this is so, then it might be morally right for five sadists who receive a total of 100 *hedons* in the process to torture a child who only suffers 50 *dolors* (antihedons). Or if a burglar will get more pleasure from my artwork than I do, he has a right to steal it (if in doing so he doesn't produce additional harm).

Sometimes utilitarians like Bentham write as if the single concern of morality was to eliminate suffering in the world. If this were morality's only concern, we would have an obligation to eliminate all sentient life as painlessly as possible, since the only way to eliminate suffering (even gratuitous suffering) is to kill every living organism.

At other times Bentham sounds as if promoting positive pleasure (and in the process eliminating pain) is the essence of morality. For this reason his version of utilitarianism was labeled "the pig philosophy" by his contemporary critics. Better a pig satisfied than Socrates dissatisfied! In an experiment done on rats electrodes are wired to the limbic areas of the cerebral cortex, and the rats are shown a button which, when pressed, will stimulate a reward or pleasure center in the brain. I'm told that the rats in the experiment become addicted to the need for the stimulation so that they lose interest in food and sex and spend most of their time pressing the stimulation button until they die. If the maximization of pleasure is what morality is all about, we ought to plug everyone, animals and humans, up to these Pleasure Machines.

Peter Singer, aware of the dangers of classic utilitarianism, has modified Bentham to present a more plausible version of utilitarianism. But the one thing in Bentham that Singer does accept is the idea that all sentient beings are linked together by their capacity to suffer. From this Singer develops his notion of Animal Liberation, a global theory of duties to animals. He has four essential points.

1. The principle of equality: that every sentient being deserves to have his or her interests given equal consideration. Each sentient being is to count for one and only for one. Status and privilege should play no part in doling out benefits. Rather we should distribute goods on the basis of need and interest.
2. The principle of utility: that the right act is the one that maximizes utility or happiness (or minimizes suffering or unhappiness).
3. Speciesism, which constitutes a violation of the principle of equality, must be rejected. Singer compares speciesism (the arbitrary favoring of one's species) with racism. "The racist . . .

[gives] greater weight to the interests of members of his own race, when there is a clash between their interests and the interests of another race. Similarly the speciesist allows the interests of his own species to override the greater interests of members of other species."[18]

4. There is a difference between our equal ability to suffer and our equal worth as rational, self-conscious agents. Here Singer separates himself from Regan who thinks all sentient beings are of equal worth. Singer values rational self-consciousness over mere sentience, but he agrees that sentience, or the ability to suffer, gives us a base line equality for some considerations.

Singer makes a distinction between activities that cause suffering and those that cause death. It may be worse to cause animals to suffer than to kill them, since the latter may be done with minimum pain and the animal generally does not have an understanding of life and death. With humans the situation is the other way around. Since humans generally prize life with pain (up to a limit) to death, it is worse to kill humans than to cause them suffering. Not all animals are of equal worth. As Singer says,[19]

A rejection of speciesism does not imply that all lives are of equal worth. While self-awareness, intelligence, the capacity for meaningful relations with others, and so on are not relevant to the question of inflicting pain—since pain is pain, whatever other capacities, beyond the capacity to feel pain, the being may have—these capacities may be relevant to the question of taking life. It is not arbitrary to hold that the life of a self-aware being, capable of abstract thought, of planning for the future, of complex acts of communication, and so on, is more valuable than the life of a being without these capacities. To see the difference between the issues of inflicting pain and taking life, consider how we would choose within our own species. If we had to choose to save the life of a normal human or a mentally defective human, we would probably choose to save the life of the normal human; but if we had to choose between preventing pain in the normal human or the mental defective— imagine that both have received painful but superficial injuries, and we only have enough painkiller for one of them—it is not nearly so clear how we ought to choose. The same is true when we consider other species. The evil of pain is, in itself, unaffected by the other characteristics of the being that feels the pain; the value of life is affected by these other characteristics.

So it is irrelevant whether animals and humans are of equal worth *when it comes to suffering.* In suffering we are to be given equal consideration. Since sentience lies at the core of our moral thinking, and language and intelligence lie nearer the periphery, a large part of our morality will have to do with liberating people and animals from suffering.

Although Singer's views are light years ahead of the other theories, they still have problems. They have some of the weaknesses attributed to Bentham—weaknesses inherent to utilitarianism—that if jealous John will suffer 100 *dolors* if he is denied my $100, but I will only suffer 80 *dolors* if he steals my $100, John has a moral right to steal my money.

Second, it's simply not obvious that if an animal is in more pain than a human we ought to give the pain reliever to the animal. In some cases this may be correct if the difference is great enough (I wouldn't rule it out automatically). The point is that if humans really are of special value, then they may deserve the painkiller even though the animal is in more pain. That is, the ability to suffer, important though it is, is not the only morally relevant property. The ability to reason, plan for the future, exercise free choice, and anticipate one's death are also significant. Finally, Singer seems peremptory in his moratorium on all but immediately relevant biomedical animal experimentation. He neglects the need for pure science, information that may be relevant to future human and animal need and which, if we don't experiment now, will be lost to future generations.

5. The Split Level Theory

The Split Level theory is the name of a position, first set forth by Martin Benjamin, that aims at correcting the above four positions.[20] The Cartesian No Status views and the Indirect Obligation view contain the insight that rational self-consciousness endows human beings with special worth, but they err on two counts: (1) in holding that animals don't have this quality at all (we know now that some do to some extent), and (2) in holding that only rational self-consciousness gives one any rights, or makes one morally considerable. At the other extreme, the Equal Status view and the Equal Consideration view recognize the importance of sentience and the ability to suffer as morally considerable, but these views tend to neglect the aspect of rational self-consciousness as setting the majority of humans apart from the majority of animals.

The Split Level view combines the insights of both types of theories. It is nonspeciesist in that it recognizes that some animals, such as chimpanzees and dolphins, may have an element of rational self-consciousness and some humans may lack it (say, fetuses and severely retarded people). The Split Level view recognizes that both sentience and rational self-consciousness are important in working out a global interspecies morality. This view rejects Regan's Sanctity of Life egalitarianism, but it also rejects Singer's equal consideration of interests principle. Rational self-consciousness does make a difference. A higher sort of being does emerge with humanity (and perhaps some higher primates and dolphins), so that we ought to treat humans with special respect.

This theory distinguishes between *trivial needs* and *important needs*. It says that with regard to important needs human needs override animal needs, but animal important needs override human trivial needs. For example, the need for sustenance and the need not to be harmed are important needs, whereas the need for having our tastes satisfied is a trivial need. So while humans have the right to kill animals if animals are necessary for health or life, we do not have the right to kill higher animals simply to satisfy our tastes. If there are equally good ways of finding nourishment, then humans have an obligation to seek those ways and permit animals to live unmolested.

The above applies to higher animals who have a developed nervous system, enabling them to suffer and develop a sense of consciousness. Since no evidence shows that termites or mosquitoes have a sense of self, it is permissible to exterminate the termites and kill the mosquitoes when they threaten our interests. If we suddenly discovered that termites and mosquitoes were highly self-conscious, we would be obliged to act differently, but until we have evidence to that effect, we may continue our present practices.

VEGETARIANISM

In the beginning of this chapter we noted some facts regarding animal mistreatment. Free-range grazing and farming has been largely replaced by the complicated technology of agribusiness, which promotes an impersonal process that tortures chicken, turkeys, cows, calves, pigs, and other animals. Since we have a moral obligation to eliminate gratuitous suffering whenever possible, we should cease to participate in the factory farming food production of our society. Rather we should oppose it. It may be moral to eat range-fed animals (and this would permit us to eat lamb and fish at present), but moral considerations, it may be argued, compel us to refuse factory-bred products—over 90 percent of the (nonfish) meat that reaches the market.

This makes good sense from an energy-conservation point of view. We would save 90 percent of nutritional energy if we abolished factory farms and ate the grain and beans now fed to the factory animals. The argument, called the Trophic Levels argument, goes like this.

No transfer of energy from one trophic level to another is 100 percent. In fact, only about 10 percent of the chemical energy available at one trophic level gets transferred and stored in usable form in the bodies of the organisms at the next trophic level. In other words, about 90 percent of the chemical energy is degraded and lost as heat to the environment. This is sometimes called the *ten percent law*. The percentage transfer of useful energy between trophic levels is called *ecologic efficiency*, or food chain efficiency. For example, suppose a man eats some grain or rice containing 10,000 units of energy. Ninety percent of the energy is lost in the transfer, so only 1000 units reach him. Now suppose that a steer eats that same grain, containing 10,000 energy units, and the steer is slaughtered and eventually fed to the man. The steer now gets the 1000 units, of which the man only gets 100 units, 90 percent of the energy being lost (as heat energy) in the transference process. Figure 8–1 illustrates this pyramid of energy in aquatic grazing systems. Original producers of food are the phytoplankton, who are eaten by zooplankton, who in turn are eaten by fish, who in turn are eaten by humans. There is a 90 percent usable energy loss (which is turned into heat) at each trophic level. In this case the fishermen only get about 10 units of energy for every 10,000 original units. It would be 1000 times more energy efficient if we could acquire a taste for phytoplankton salad!

Decreased efficiency occurs as we move from the primary producers of food to the consumers. We would get a lot more food value if we ate the beans, lentils, nuts, and grains that animals ate rather than the

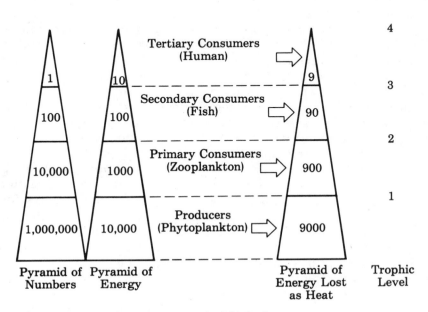

FIGURE 8–1   *The pyramid of energy and trophic levels.*

animals themselves. More than 80 or 90 percent of food energy could be saved in the process.

So modest vegetarianism is both rational and moral. There are no compelling reasons for prohibiting eating farm animals, provided that they are not tortured and that they die with as little pain as possible. Lamb, deer, and free-range animals may be eaten—though in small quantities—for there is no loss of nutritional energy in these cases (we cannot digest the grass eaten by these animals). Of course, if grazing land could be used to grow food crops, that would be a consideration against animal grazing. Mary Ann Warren has pointed out that there may be environmental reasons for refraining from grazing free-range animals, for they greatly damage the ecology of fragile arid lands. She writes, "It might be better to do less grazing of domestic animals on marginal land, and go on feeding some animals with grain."[21] These qualifications need to be taken into consideration in a case by case assessment of situations. Since fish in open waters are plentiful and are not caused inordinate suffering, we can continue to eat them—although there may be reasons to prohibit factory farming of fish. For the rest, we ought to learn to adjust our palates to vegetables, grains, beans, lentils, and fruit.

ANIMAL EXPERIMENTS

We noted that millions of animals die in laboratory experiments each year. Richard Ryder puts the figure between 100 and 300 million worldwide.[22] Many of these experiments are unnecessary and unjustified. More needs to be done to avoid unnecessary duplication and to enforce the laws requiring the use of anesthetics. Andrew Rowan and others have argued that alternative, nonanimal testing procedures, such as CAT and PET scans, in vitro cell and tissue cultures, and autopsy studies, can reduce or replace animal experiments in many instances. For example, CAT and PET scans have been valuable in the study of Parkinson's disease, visual physiology, and musculoskeletal tumors.[23]

Nevertheless, Regan's principle of rejecting all animal experimentation is to be rejected. Most proponents of alternative nonanimal testing procedures concede that the cessation of animal experimentation now or in the foreseeable future would have adverse consequences for humans. If we accept the Split Level theory, as I have argued we should, then experimentation with safeguards should continue.

It is vitally important that we eliminate or control serious disease (AIDS, cancer, heart disease), and to do this animal experiments are often necessary. Medical research on animals has helped bring about treatment of diabetes, cancer, stroke, and heart ailments. "Dogs were used in the discovery of insulin and monkeys were used in the development of a polio vaccine."[24] We have no reason to believe that we can discover treatments for many diseases without experimenting on animals. If so, we should use every safeguard in preventing abuse as we carry out our experiments. Most, if not all, university research centers now have institutional animal care and use committees to review and approve experimental protocols. But we can eliminate animal experiments in testing cosmetics, football helmets, and other items not vital to human flourishing. Either do without these luxuries (cosmetics and football helmets—we might have to resort to "touch-football") or find other ways of testing the products.

Singer, more moderate than Regan, would accept that some experimentation is justified. "Experiments serving no direct and urgent purpose should stop immediately, and in the remaining areas of research, methods involving animals should be replaced as soon as possible by alternative methods not involving animals."[25] But this may be too restrictive. It may be necessary to do some animal experiments simply to understand how organisms function. This is sometimes referred to as *basic research*. Basic research may be prima facie justified for its own sake, but it may also become valuable for discovering cures to diseases. Henry Sackin has pointed out[26]:

> Very often we simply do not know whether a path of scientific inquiry will ultimately lead to something important or useful. [Such basic reasearch as that which led to] the discovery of the structure of DNA in 1953 would have been regarded by animal advocates as inappropriate and irrelevant. Yet it forms the basis of molecular biology that now makes it possible to genetically engineer pest resistant crops and provide adequate and inexpensive insulin for diabetics. Only those of us who possess divine omniscience can argue that certain animal experiments are less important than others. We simply do not know what is or is not important until after we understand the implications of that knowledge. This may explain why Nobel prizes are often awarded years after the original discoveries were actually made.

HUNTING FOR SPORT, FURS, ZOOS, AND RODEOS

Hunting for necessary food is morally permissible, and in some cases hunting may be warranted in keeping the animal population down, but hunting primarily for sport, trophies, or the fun of killing are activities much harder to justify from a moral perspective.

If furs are necessary for people to keep warm, we may legitimately kill animals for their furs, but if less violent ways of producing clothes are available, we should take them. If we can produce good synthetic shoes, we should begin using them instead of leather shoes. Leather sofas and coats probably are not morally acceptable since we can produce good quality sofas and coats in other ways.

Zoos may be the only way people learn about animals, so that they may be morally acceptable, but conditions must be such that animals benefit from these conditions. They must be treated kindly.

CONCLUSION

All conscious beings are morally considerable, since they can suffer and be aided in flourishing; but, unless we want to stop killing harmful (to us) bacteria, we can agree that some animals are more valuable than others. Those who have a sense of personal identity, who are rationally self-conscious, and have plans and projects, deserve special consideration. So the Split Level view seems, on balance, to be the correct position. Regarding important needs, human needs in general override the needs of lower animals, but regarding trivial needs, the important needs of animals override these nonvital needs of humans. Speciesism is a vice, like racism, if it causes irrational privilege to humans simply because they are human, but because humanity as a species is superior to other species, no evil is involved in developing general policies that reflect that fact.

The basic principle that should be at work in our relations with animals is the Principle of Nonmaleficence. We ought not to cause unnecessary harm or suffering. Is there a better way to live and eat? If so, then we should take it. Do we need to do all the research and animal experimentation in which we are presently engaged? If not, we should cut out the unnecessary experimentation. Are hunting and trapping necessary for human flourishing? If not, we should work toward the elimination of these activities. For the rest, we should be kind to all the creatures of the earth, trying to make this cruel jungle into the Garden of Eden.

Look again at Regan's three goals: (1) The total abolition of the use of animals in science; (2) the total dissolution of commercial animal agriculture; and (3) the total elimination of commercial and sport hunting and trapping. If the Split Level analysis is correct, all these goals may be rejected as absolutist, but each has a point. Abuses must be eliminated in research, and animal factories must be abolished. Hunting and trapping for sport or furs should in general be prohibited, but exceptions might be permitted—for example, when a deer population is reaching a dangerous surplus and a die back is likely.

Schematically put, here are the results of our analysis:

Justified Activities

1. Free-range animals, especially if they are necessary for a community's well-being or survival. Note that cows and goats eat grasses that are not digestible by humans, so that no energy loss occurs in eating these cows and goats.
2. Important biomedical experiments to increase scientific knowledge and find cures for diseases. But safeguards must be built into these experiments, minimizing the harm done to the animals. While some basic research is warranted, unnecessay duplication should be prevented.
3. Zoos to enable city dwellers to learn about animals. They must meet minimum standards of decency for animals.
4. Hunting for food or when an animal population gets out of control.

Activities Not Justified

1. Animal factories, where the suffering of animals is terrible and unnecessary.
2. Nonvital experimentation, such as cosmetic experiments and football helmets.
3. Other luxury activities where animals are unnecessarily exploited, such as hunting for sport or fur, and bullfights.

At the end of *Animal Liberation*, Singer issues a challenge for us all[27]:

Human beings have the power to continue to oppress other species forever, or until we make this planet unsuitable for living beings. Will our tyranny continue, proving that we really are the selfish tyrants that the most cynical of the poets and philosophers have always said we are? Or will we rise to the challenge and prove our capacity for genuine altruism by ending our ruthless exploitation of the species in our power, not because we are forced to do so by rebels or terrorists, but because we recognize that our position is morally indefensible?

While we have warrant for using some animals for human good, we ought to modify many of our practices, realizing that animals have interests and are morally significant.

Study Questions

1. Discuss the two quotations at the head of this chapter. Are either of them true or close to the truth? Explain.

2. What are the implications of the moral principle "Do no unnecessary harm"? Would it lead us to abolish factory farming? eating meat? some animal experimentation? all animal experimentation? hunting? Explain your position.

3. Discuss the five theories on the moral status of animals outlined in this chapter. Which position seems the best to you? Would that position call for changes in your actions?

4. Is it morally permissible to eat meat? Under what circumstances would it be moral or immoral?

5. Discuss the arguments for vegetarianism. How does the trophic pyramid affect your thinking about using animals for food?

6. Is hunting for sport morally permissible? Consider the following description of a hunter's killing an elephant:

> The elephant stood broadside to me, at upwards of one hundred yards, and his attention at the moment was occupied with the dogs. . . . I fired at his shoulder, and secured him with a single shot. The ball caught him high on the shoulder-blade, rendering him instantly lame; and before the echo on the bullet could reach my ear, I plainly saw the elephant was mine. . . . I resolved to devote a short time to the contemplation of this noble elephant before laying him low; . . . I quickly kindled a fire and put on the kettle, and in a few minutes my coffee was prepared. There I sat in my forest home, cooly sipping my coffee, with one of the finest elephants in Africa awaiting my pleasure beside a neighboring tree . . .
>
> Having admired the elephant for a considerable time, I resolved to make experiments for vulnerable points . . . [the hunter misses the vulnerable points, further wounding the elephant, but finally he succeeds in delivering a fatal shot]. Large tears now trickled from [the elephant's] eyes, which he slowly shut and opened, his colossal frame quivered convulsively, and falling on his side, he expired." (Quoted in Richard Carrington, *Elephants*. New York: Chatto and Windus, 1958, p. 158).

Discuss the moral significance of this act.

7. It has been argued by Robert White and many others that without experimentation on animals the cures for many diseases would not have been discovered. Does this justify animal experimentation? Explain.

Endnotes

1. The Office of Technological Assessment (OTA) put the number of animals produced for laboratory experiments each year between 35 and 50 million. Andrew Rowan, who has made one of the most thorough studies of

the matter, told me that he had down-scaled his estimate from between 60 and 70 million animals to a figure close to that of the OTA. For helpful discussions of the scientific literature on the ethics of animal research see M. T. Phillips and J. A. Sechzer, *Animal Research and Ethical Conflict* (New York: Springer-Verlag, 1989) and Andrew Rowan, *Of Mice, Models and Men: A Critical Evaluation of Animal Research* (Albany, N.Y.: State University of New York Press, 1984).

2. The material in this section on animal experimentation is taken from Richard Ryder's *Victims of Science: The Use of Animals in Research* (London: National Anti-Vivisection Society, 1983); Andrew Rowan, op. cit.; Peter Singer, *Animal Liberation*, 2nd ed. (New York Review of Books, 1990); Muriel the Lady Dowding, "Furs and Cosmetics: Too High a Price?" in Stanley and Rosline Godlovitch and John Harris, eds., *Animals, Men and Morals* (New York: Taplinger Publishing, 1972), and Phillip Zwerling, "Animal Rights, Human Wrongs," *Animal Agenda* (December 1985).

3. Singer, op. cit., pp. 29f. Other reports tell of dogs that are driven insane with electric shocks so that scientists can study the effects of insanity. Cats are deprived of sleep until they die. Primates have been restrained for months in steel chairs allowing no movement, and elephants have been given LSD to study aggression. Legs have been cut off mice to study how they walk on the stumps, and polar bears have been drowned in vats of crude oil to study the effect of oil spills in polar regions.

4. Singer, op. cit., p. 80. Researchers Henry Sackin and Jeri Sechzer of Cornell Medical College have assured me that many of the abuses in animal experimentation have been halted in recent years owing to the surveillance of institutional review committees. Others, like Steven Kaufman of the Medical Research Modernization Committee, argue that abuses still abound. Peter Singer documents that in the international scientific community the United States has a reputation for failing to enforce reasonable standards in animal experimentation. In the New York City offices of United Action for Animals there are filing cabinets full of photocopies of experiments under the labels of "Burning," "Concussion," "Crushing," "Experimental Neurosis," "Freezing," "Heating," "Radiation," "Starvation," "Shock," and "Spinal Cord Injuries." Singer, op. cit., pp. 65f; 79f.

5. The material in this paragraph is based on John Robbins' *Diet for a New America* (Walpole, N.H.: Stillpoint Publishing, 1987).

6. James Rachels, "Vegetarianism," in *World Hunger and Moral Obligation*, William Aiken and Hugh LaFollette, eds. (Englewood Cliffs, N.J.: Prentice Hall, 1977), pp. 180–93.

7. René Descartes, *Discourse on Method*, in *The Philosophical Works of Descartes*, Haldane and Ross, trans. (Cambridge: Cambridge University Press, 1911) vol. I.

8. William Whewell, *Lectures*, p. 223, cited in *Animal Rights and Human Obligations*, Peter Singer and Tom Regan, eds. (Englewood Cliffs, N.J.: Prentice Hall, 1976) p. 131.

9. Cited in M. T. Phillips and J. Sechzer, op. cit., p. 75f.

10. Ibid, p. 75f.

11. Thomas Aquinas, *Summa Theologica* (London: Benziger Brothers, 1918), Part II, Question 64, Article 1.

12. Thomas Aquinas, *Contra Gentiles* (London: Benziger Brothers, 1928), Third Book, Part II, Ch. CXII.

13. Immanuel Kant, *Lectures on Ethics*, Louis Infield, trans. (New York: Harper & Row, 1963), p. 239.

14. K. McCabe, "Who Will Live, Who Will Die," *The Washingtonian* (August, 1986) and "Beyond Cruelty," op. cit. (February 1990).

15. Tom Regan, "The Case for Animal Rights," in *In Defense of Animals*, Peter Singer, ed. (Oxford: Blackwell, 1985), pp. 13–26.

16. Ibid, p. 13.

17. Jeremy Bentham, *The Principles of Morals and Legislation* (1789), ch XVII, Section 1.

18. Peter Singer, *Animal Liberation* (New York: Avon, 1976), p. 108.

19. Ibid, pp. 21, 22. In another place Singer puts his point this way: "There are many areas in which the superior mental powers of normal adult humans make a difference: anticipation, more detailed memory, greater knowledge of what is happening, and so on. These differences explain why a human dying from cancer is likely to suffer more than a mouse. It is the mental anguish which makes the human's position so much harder to bear. Yet these differences do not all point to greater suffering on the part of the normal human being. Sometimes animals may suffer *more* because of their more limited understanding. If, for instance, we are taking prisoners in wartime we can explain to them that while they must submit to capture, search, and confinement they will not otherwise be harmed and will be set free at the conclusion of hostilities. If we capture a wild animal, however, we cannot explain that we are not threatening its life. A wild animal cannot distinguish an attempt to overpower and confine from an attempt to kill; the one causes as much terror as the other." (Singer, *Practical Ethics* [Cambridge: Cambridge University Press, 1979], p. 53.)

20. Martin Benjamin, "Ethics and Animal Consciousness" in *Social Ethics*, Thomas Mappes and Jane Zembaty, eds. (Englewood Cliffs, N.J.: Prentice-Hall, 1982)

21. Mary Anne Warren in correspondence, January 25, 1991.

22. Ryder, op. cit., p. 26.

23. Rowan, op. cit., p. 261, and The Medical Research Modernization Committee Report, "A Critical Look at Animal Research" (New York: MRMC, 1990). See also *Perspectives on Animal Research* of the Medical Research Modernization Committee, which has given further examples.

24. Henry Sackin, "An Ethical Basis for Animal Experimentation" (unpublished paper). Many would take issue with Sackin's claim that "the discovery of the structure of DNA in 1953 would have been regarded by animal advocates as inappropriate and irrelevant."

25. Singer, op cit., p. 32.

26. Sackin, op cit.

27. Singer, op cit., p. 258.

CHAPTER 9

War

Nothing is worth dying for.

—PLACARD AT AN AMERICAN ANTIWAR RALLY

Strive against (jihad) the infidels and the hypocrites! Be harsh with them. Their ultimate destiny is hell.

—THE KORAN 9:73

War is a means of resolving conflicts of interest by other than rational persuasion. In war two groups resort to violence to settle differences. War is bloody, destructive, vile, and irrational, but it has been humanity's most startling way of asserting power and struggling to survive. I remember meeting a devout Catholic woman on board the Norwegian Liner the "Bergenfjord," in 1971 as I sailed back from Denmark to the United States. She was expressing outrage at the decadence and secularity of our times and criticized Planned Parenthood and our whole contraceptive culture as *"man's* faithless means to prevent overpopulation." "We have no faith in God," she said regarding this aspect of social policy. "Why, God has always had His methods of population control." I asked what they were. "War, Famine, and Disease," she exclaimed, wondering how I could be so stupid as to have to ask. "Maybe 'man's faithless means' are better," I meekly offered.

Famine and disease, whether we want to blame God for them or not, have been scourges on humanity, but the means of destruction for which we may take peculiar credit is war. We seem mysteriously, almost religiously, addicted to this sadomasochistic enterprise. Why is this so? Why do we love the blood-dipped sword?

WAR IN WESTERN HISTORY:
FROM MOSES TO THE PRESENT

The history of humanity is the story of violence, bloodshed, pillage, massacre, and plunder. What is more, it is the story of the *glorification* of violence, bloodshed, pillage, massacre, and plunder. Witness the military symbols in national anthems, the marches and parades in honor of past wars (for example, Veteran's Day marches and the parades honoring soldiers from the recent war with Iraq), the sense of pride in victory, the making of the military hero, and the dehumanizing of the enemy. All this is part of the litany of lust for carnage and conquest that has haunted our history. The slain victims are seen not as the cannon fodder of megalomaniacs and incompetents but as heroes wreathed in immortality. Marble monuments in a thousand marketplaces mark their memory. The war tax is usually the highest item in a nation's budget and frequently the only tax people do not hesitate to pay—witness the sudden influx of money to the government of Argentina (a land where collecting taxes is well-nigh impossible) during the Falkland Islands War, while Argentinia was supposed to be on the edge of bankruptcy. While the United States lacks funds to improve its inner cities and lift millions out of poverty, it finds the needed resources to fight a war a long way from its shores.

Only recently, our hearts were riveted by the spectacle of courage and genius in the service of death and destruction against the Iraquis in Kuwait. The answer to the question of why war is so attractive is that it brings all human talents and energies to their highest tension and sets a crown of immortality on those who courageously risk their lives and conquer. The very danger and horror of the moment is its thrill.

Homo sapiens is one of the few species that systematically kills members of its own species. Because of this and because of the threat of attack by rivals, societies deem defense systems necessary for their survival. Note that over 90 percent of all nations that have ever existed have been destroyed, often because they have not been militarily strong enough to defend themselves. From Shalmaneser III of Assyria to President Gorbachev and President Bush, the need for a strong defense has been duly recognized. The problem is that the "defensive" army all too frequently becomes offensive.

Some 93 major wars occurred in the 150 years between 1816 and 1965 (about seven per decade), and 75 wars (not all major) have taken place in the past 40 years. About 40,000 people are killed every month in a war. In the American Civil War more than 600,000 Americans lost their lives. In World War II between 40 and 50 million people were killed. In the Viet Nam War a million Vietnamese and 57,000 Americans died. Death and destruction have been the hallmarks of human history. From the very onset of our culture this was so.

In the Old Testament, Israel, with Yahweh's approval, pursues genocidal war. The foundations of Israel were laid in the destruction of Pharaoh's army and the Egyptian first-born. God hardened Pharaoh's heart so that He could destroy him, and when the Israelites pledged themselves to Yahweh as His chosen people, the covenant they dedicated themselves to included a prohibition against murder and a prescription in favor of annihilating their neighbors. "When my angel goes before you and brings you in to the Amorites, and the Hittites, and the Perizzites, and the Canaanites, the Hivites, and the Jebusites, and I blot them out, you shall not bow down to their gods, nor serve them. . . . I will send my terror before you, and will throw into confusion all the people against whom you come, and I will make all your enemies turn their backs to you. . . . You shall make no covenant with them or with their gods" (Ex 23:23-32). The Psalmist, who can sing Zion's songs of praise to God with one breath, can sing the doom of revenge in the next: "O daughter of Babylon, you devastator! Happy shall he be who requites you with what you have done to us! Happy shall he be who takes your little ones and dashes them against the rocks" (Ps 137:8, 9). Jehovah is a god of blood and thunder, His people the people of the sword. The *jihad* doesn't begin with Islam but is already found in the Hebrew Bible with Israel.

The Greeks are no better. The *Iliad* is one long recital of how Diomedes, Ajax, Sarpedon, Achilles, and Hector killed. Greek history, as William James rightly tells us, is a "panorama of jingoism and imperialism—war for war's sake, all the citizens being warriors. . . . Their wars were purely piratical. Pride, gold, women, slaves, excitement, were their only motives."[1] The Spartans, led by one of the greatest military geniuses of all time, Lycurgus, were the paradigm of a military state, in which everyone, male and female, learned to kill from childhood. So keen on war did they become that peace posed a threat to their social cohesion.

During the Peloponnesian war in the fifth century B.C. the Athenians asked the inhabitants of Melos, hitherto neutral, to acknowledge their lordship. The envoys meet and hold a debate, which Thucydides gives in full, and which for sweet reasonableness of form stands out in candor and eloquence. The Melians demur and say that they refuse to be slaves. They appeal to the gods for help.

The Athenian general replies: "The powerful exact what they can and the weak grant what they must. Of the gods we believe and of men we know that by a law of nature, wherever they can rule, they will. This law was not made by us, and we know that you and all mankind, if you were as strong as we are, would do as we do. So much for the gods; we have told you why we expect to stand as high in their good opinions as you."[2]

Thereupon the Athenians put to death all who were of military age and made slaves of the women and children. They then colonized the island, sending thither 500 Athenian settlers.

The Greeks gave us the notion of *Realpolitik*—kill or be killed; conquer or die. War no longer is seen as divinely inspired but as a mechanism for survival and power in which the Brazen Rule predates the Golden Rule—"Do it to others before they get a chance to do it to you."

In the New Testament Jesus advocates pacifism in the Sermon on the Mount. "Love your enemies. Do not resist evil. If someone strikes you on the right cheek, turn to him the other also." The early Christians were pacifists and generally refused to serve in the Roman army. In the second century Tertullian summed up the Christian position on military service. "There is no agreement between the divine and human sacrament, the standard of Christ and the standard of the devil, the camp of light and the camp of darkness. One soul cannot belong to two lords-God and Caesar." Regarding Peter's use of the sword on the night of Judas's betrayal of Jesus, Tertullian writes, "The Lord in disarming Peter, unbelted every soldier."[3]

However, once the Church came to power, it changed its mind and reinterpreted the message of Christ to apply to saints. The beatitudes and Sermon on the Mount consisted in "Councils of Perfection," not strict duties. Augustine (354–430) developed the idea of a just war. The Crusades were launched against Islam, Catholic and Protestant have killed each other in the name of God, and a presumption of God's approval has accompanied warriors against those of other creeds. Christian civilization has wielded the sword as readily and deftly as others.

Historically, within Western culture there have been three major philosophic attitudes toward war: romanticism, abolitionism, and realism. The War-Romantics believed that war is good for humanity in that it purges the dross of society, so that only the fit survive, and it brings out the best in humanity: courage, perseverance, knife-edge concentration, endurance, resilience, heroism, and intelligence. Hegel believed that war cleanses the nation and that humanity must accept war or stagnate. Napoleon spoke of war as glorious. Nietzsche said, "a good war hallows every cause." War is a natural activity that opposes Christianity with its slave morality, "accentuating humility, submissiveness and turning of the cheek." Helmut von Moltke put it this way[4]:

Perpetual Peace is a dream—and not even a beautiful dream—War is an integral part of God's ordering of the Universe. In War man's noblest virtues come into play: courage and renunciation, fidelity to duty and a readiness for sacrifice that does not stop short of offering up Life itself. Without War the World would become swamped in materialism.

Similarly, Von Treitschke wrote, "The state's first duty is to maintain its power in relation to other states—war is the one remedy for an ailing nation."[5] War is the process by which the truly civilized nations express their strength and vitality; life is an unending struggle for survival, war is an instrument in biologic evolution, killing off the less fit. Von Treitschke, with his racist tones, is the philosopher who inspired the Italian Fascists and German Nazis.

War is manly, strong, and brave; peace is feminine, weak, and defeatist. The *jihad* will bring immortal glory. Look at the quotations at the beginning of this chapter and contrast the protestor's pusillanimous placard with the misguided message of determined courage conveyed by the Koran. The first signifies the triumph of banality, the leveling of values, for if *nothing* is worth dying for, can anything be worth living for? While the passage from the Koran seems to enjoin fanaticism, at least it signifies a commitment to the good and true. That is the one truth in the romantic's message: life is serious and our deepest values are worth preserving even to death.

We turn to the Abolitionists with the question, Is war inevitable or can we replace it with a lasting peace? Abolitionists argue that the abolition of war is possible and that we should assume the attitude of peace and nonviolence now. As we noted earlier, the early Christians were persecuted pacifists. But after the Emperor Constantine saw the vision of the cross at the battle of the Milvian Bridge and made Christianity the official religion of the Roman Empire (A.D. 313), Christians promptly embarked on a policy of persecuting heretics and battling infidels. Under Augustine pacifism gave way to the concept of the just war, which we will examine shortly. Nevertheless, the Abolitionist tradition perdured as a minority voice in the choir of theology from Erasmus to George Fox and the Quakers to the Roman Catholic Bishop of Atlanta. Erasmus condemned the use of war as a great evil that opposes everything that humans have been created for. Men and women are born not for destruction, but for love, friendship, and service to fellow humans. Kant wrote a guide to the commencement of perpetual peace. Bertrand Russell conceded that, if it came to that, we are better red than dead. Tolstoy, Gandhi, and Martin Luther King Jr. practiced nonviolent resistance in the name of pacifism, proving that it could achieve more than some might have expected. Pacifism is reemerging in our country as a serious option. The Roman Catholic Bishop of Atlanta has said that in a nuclear age there is no such thing as a just war. In a recent, well-acclaimed study, *On War and Morality* (1989), the philosopher Robert Holmes argues that because innocents are killed in war, the whole enterprise of war is immoral and cannot be justified.

While these sentiments are praiseworthy, there are serious problems both with pacifism itself and with the argument from innocence in particular.

Pacifism holds that it is immoral to engage in war even to defend yourself from attack. The problem with this is that on one hand, pacifism tells us not to kill others because they have a right to life, while on the other hand it tells us that we may not defend our right to life even against evil attacks! This is a strange kind of *right* that cannot be defended.

We may put the argument this way.

1. All humans (qua innocent) have the right not to be treated violently.
2. If we have any rights at all, we have the right to use force to prevent the deprivation of the thing to which we have a right.
3. Pacifism says both that we have some rights and that we may not use force to protect them.

But what is a *right* if we do not have the *right* to protect it? The very notion of a right entails an accompanying liberty to defend it for oneself and for others. The pacifist's logic is confused, its doctrine incoherent.[6]

Of course, having a right to defend our right to life doesn't require us to defend it. You can sacrifice your own right to life or right to protect your life, but what you cannot do is require others to sacrifice their right to prevent the unauthorized abrogation of their right to life. Further, you may have a duty to defend other people's right to life by preventive measures.

To what lengths may we go to defend our right to life? Here the notion of proportionality comes in. We may use just enough force to get the job done. But if the only way to defend a right to life against an aggressor is to kill the aggressor, that act is morally justified.

Applying this to war: if it's moral to defend your family, friends, or innocent people from an assailant by killing the assailant, then it's moral to defend your country or another friendly country from being taken over by an aggressor by attacking that aggressor.

If we have to kill some shields (innocent people or hostages placed in front of the aggressors) to save our family, then we may justifiably kill innocent people in the enemy country, if that is the only way to get to the aggressor.

Remember, the pacifist's claim is not that we *may* give up our right to self-defense, but that we morally *must* give it up. It is immoral to kill the aggressor who is torturing our children or about to blow up a bus with innocent civilians on it, even if killing him or her is the only way to save these innocent people.

Of course, Jesus and the early Christians held to pacifism with a difference. They held that this life was not worth defending because it was only the gateway to a better life, and the sooner we get there the better. On this logic the murderer does his victim a favor, so there is no reason to resist violence. If people believe this, pacifism may make sense, but given that most of us have doubts about immortality and would like to make this world as just as possible, pacifism will not have a lot to recommend it.

The pacifist argues that his or her position has the advantage that if it were universalized, there would be no war. But this is shortsighted. We could also universalize the thesis "Never go to war unless another nation is seriously threatening to attack you" and still obtain the same results: a principle that, if universally followed, would prohibit war.

A weaker version of pacifism argues that while we may defend ourselves and others against personal violence directly, war is never morally justified because it involves the killing of innocent people. Richard Wasserstrom states the argument this way[7]:

> Even in war innocent persons have a right to life and limb that should be respected. It is no less wrong and no more justifiable to kill innocent persons in war than at any other time. Therefore, if innocent persons are killed in a war, that war is to be condemned. The argument can quite readily be converted into an attack upon all modern war. Imagine a thoroughly unprovoked attack upon another country—an attack committed, moreover, from the worst of motives and for the most despicable of ends. Assume too, for the moment, that under such circumstances there is nothing immoral about fighting back and even killing those who are attacking. Nonetheless, if in fighting back innocent persons will be killed, the defenders will be acting immorally. However, given any war fought today, innocent persons will inevitably be killed. Therefore, any war fought today will be immoral.

The argument may be analyzed in this form.

1. Killing innocents is immoral.
2. In war innocents are killed.
3. Therefore, war is immoral.

The argument is fallacious, committing the fallacy of composition: faulty reasoning from the part to the whole. For example: "Every atom in the Empire State Building is so small as to be invisible to the naked eye. Since the Empire State Building is composed entirely of atoms, it must be so small as to be invisible to the naked eye." Or "Every person in America has a mother. Therefore, America has a mother." Just because parts of war are immoral doesn't mean that the whole is immoral. There are abuses in business, sports, education, families, and government, but that doesn't mean that on the whole business, sports, education, families, and government are evil. They may be moral without being morally perfect.

There is no absolute purity in this life, no absolute good in human activity, and to make that a precondition for any activity is to condemn oneself to inaction.

We need to appreciate the principle of the *Lesser Evil.* Tragic situations occur in which no pure good is available. Recall the trolley car example from Chapter 5. Noticing that the brakes of the trolley car have failed, you, the driver, have the choice between doing nothing and allowing five workmen to die and turning the trolley off onto a spur where you will kill one person. Either way, someone will die. Not to choose is still to choose. It is to choose to allow the greater evil to take place for which you are responsible. Likewise, recall Sophie's tragic choice in William Styron's *Sophie's Choice*, where the young inmate of the Nazi concentration camp must choose between sacrificing her son and her daughter. Otherwise, the Nazis will execute both children. Moral choice sometimes means doing evil, when it is the lesser of evils in a situation where all options result in evil.

If Romanticism and Abolitionism are invalid positions, Realism will seem attractive. While some realists have cynically opted for a theory of total war with no holds barred ("All's fair in love and war"), most realists, believing that human sinfulness made war inevitable, advocate mitigating constraints, aiming to limit the damage. Realists are to be distinguished from the War-Romantics, for they do not like war but see it as a necessary evil. Machiavelli thought that war was inevitable not because humans were evil (he thought humanity was weak and stupid, not evil) but because of the activity of malign fate, which is always forcing humans to arm themselves against adversity. Machiavelli held out no hope that war raised humanity to a higher plane; the prince is condemned to seek victory in war merely to survive in a hostile world. In peace a ruler should not sit with hands folded but should always be improving his state's military power against the day of adversity.

Thomas Hobbes (1588–1679) thought that war is not the act of fighting but the disposition to fight that exists in situations in which no common superior ensures that violence shall not be permitted. Only through the establishment of a commonwealth (that is, a superior law-enforcing agency, the *Leviathan,* to which all people are subject) can war be avoided and peace and civilization be ensured.

MORALITY AND THE JUST WAR

Given the broadly realist conception of war it remains to examine ways of mitigating the violence through moral constraints. Three classic theories of morality—Utilitarianism, Contractualism, and Deontologism—prescribe three different strategies. Utilitarian theories, which seek to maximize goodness ("The greatest good for the greatest number"), enjoin a cost–benefit analysis to determine the likely outcomes of diverse strategies. When nations are in conflict, war becomes one option that may be considered as a means of conflict resolution. The only question to be asked is, "How likely is it that war will bring about a better total outcome than any alternative policy?" If after careful analysis war is judged likely to bring about the greatest total benefit, then war is justified.

A *Realpolitik* prevails. No civilian–combatant distinction exists. If you can accomplish more by killing civilians, you are justified in so doing, though this may set off a bad precedent in killing civilians—so be careful! The decision to drop the atom bomb on Hiroshima was justified from a utilitarian perspective. Reflect upon the words of President Truman[8]:

> Having found the bomb, we have to use it. We have used it against those who attacked us without warning at Pearl Harbor, against those who have starved and beaten and executed American prisoners of war, against those who have abandoned all pretense of obeying international laws of warfare. We have used it in order to shorten the agony of war, in order to save the lives of thousands and thousands of young Americans.

Assuming that more good will be done by sacrificing the enemy lives to American lives, the argument has utilitarian traits. Save lives by killing others.

Of course, Truman's reasoning could also be construed as simply enlightened self-interest, a view held by contractualist types of ethics. According to the contractualist, war is justified for a country whenever that country's self-interest is to go to war. Egoist-enlightened self-interest is the leitmotif of contractualism, which leads nations into treaties. Once bound to treaties, the nations may support one another in battle. Where no contract exists, no moral obligation exists, and where a contract exists the obligation must be surrounded with sanctions. Otherwise, the treaty is void, for, as Hobbes noted, "covenants without the sword are but words, and of no strength to secure man at all." Generally, if it is in a country's self-interest to make a treaty that includes the promise to defend another country, that treaty should be adhered to, for you will probably need that country's aid in the future, and backing out of a treaty is a poor advertisement to others. So if our government has a treaty with Saudi Arabia, Kuwait, or Israel, we should honor it and defend these countries when they are attacked or threatened. Interestingly enough, the United States had no treaty with Kuwait when it went to that country's aid.

As was the case with utilitarian theory, contractual theory recognizes no special rule distinguishing civilians from combatants. All are fair game.

We turn to Deontologic Ethics and the famous Just War theory. Augustine (354 – 430), Thomas Aquinas (1225 –1274), and Francisco Suarez (1548 –1617), a Roman Catholic Jesuit in the Middle Ages, believed that war, although an evil, could be justified if certain conditions were met. As deontologists, they reject simple cost–benefit calculations and the whole notion of total war—that all is fair in love and war. They distinguished between moral grounds for going into war (*jus ad bellum*) and right conduct while engaged in war (*jus in bello*). *Jus ad bellum*, the right to go to war, could be justified by the following circumstances. The war must be:

1. Declared by a legitimate authority. This would rule out revolutionary wars and rebel uprisings.
2. Declared for a just cause. The allies World War II declaration of war on the Japanese and Germans, who were seen as bent on destroying Western democracy, is often cited as the paradigm case of such a just declaration of war. The recent war against Iraq was allegedly about the integrity of Kuwait as well as the danger to Saudi Arabia, Syria, and, especially, Israel. It was also about the control of oil in the Middle East.
3. Declared as a last resort. Belligerency may commence only after a reasonable determination has been made that war is the only way to accomplish good ends. In the recent war against Iraq people argued that serious efforts at negotiation had failed and that sanctions were not working, so that war was the only alternative.
4. Declared with the intention of bringing peace and holding respect (and even love) for the enemy. The opposition must be respected as human beings even as we attack them.

Note that the Just War theory permits preemptive strikes if the leaders are certain of intended aggression—as in Israel's Six Days' War in 1967.

Regarding carrying on the war (*Jus in bello*) two further conditions are given.

5. Proportionality. The war must be carried out in moderation, exacting no more casualties than are necessary for accomplishing the good end. No more force than necessary to achieve the just goal may be exercised. Pillage, rape, and torture are forbidden. There is no justification for cruel treatment of innocents, prison-

ers, and the wounded. Nuclear war seems to violate the principle of proportionality.

6. Discrimination. Contrary to utilitarian and contractualist theories, the Just War theory makes a distinction between combatants and noncombatants—those deemed innocent in the fray. It is impermissible to attack nonmilitary targets and noncombatants. Civilian bombing is outlawed by international law. The massacre of civilians at My Lai was seen as the nadir of despicable behavior by American forces in the Viet Nam War.

While there is much to commend this kind of reasoning, and in the end it may be close to what an adequate moral view of war would come up with, it seems more applicable to a confined Medieval battlefield with knights on horses, voluntarily engaging the enemy in the name of the king, than to the modern world where political legitimacy is often open to question, where conscription may force young men and women to do a dictator's bidding, where the whole infrastructure of a nation may be relevant to the outcome, and where the enemy does not abide by the rules of proportionality or discrimination.

While few would question conditions 2, 3, and 4, since they seem self-evidently necessary to doing any lesser evil, utilitarians would urge us to reject the sixth condition, discrimination. If by bombing a city in which 10,000 civilian lives were lost we could save 15,000 soldiers, we should bomb the city. Whatever does the least total evil should be done, never mind the individual rules.

Where the utilitarian wavers is when practices such as torture are considered. If we could save 10 of our soldiers by torturing one enemy soldier, should we do it? Is torture one of those unspeakable evils that should transcend (or nearly transcend) the utilitarian calculus? Perhaps utilitarianism is plausible when comparing lives but not when heinous acts like torture are involved. But then is torture really any worse than mass killing, leaving children orphans, or using nuclear weapons to accomplish purposes of state?

The distinction between innocents (noncombatants) and combatants is especially problematic. What if the civilians are shields for the combatants? Do you refrain from killing the enemy who is threatening you on the basis of not intending to kill the shield?

An analogy may be helpful. If a murderer who is using a hostage as a shield is about to kill you and your family, and you may save your family only by shooting the hostage as well as the murderer, is it morally permissible to shoot the hostage? Just War theory would say No, but this is doubtful. For the utilitarian the first five conditions may be rules of thumb that help in the decision of whether to go to war, but the final condition is arbitrary.

NUCLEAR WAR

Whatever your conclusion on which moral theory deals best with war, the threat of nuclear war puts the very concept of a Just War in serious doubt. Consider the facts. The atomic bomb that fell on Hiroshima on August 6, 1945, killing 60,000 people, had an explosive force of 12,000 tons of TNT. The nuclear warhead on an American Minuteman missile has an explosive force of 1.2 million tons of TNT, 100 times the force of the bomb that fell on Hiroshima. A larger 10-megaton hydrogen bomb has an explosive force 800 times that of the Hiroshima bomb. The United States and the former Soviet Union together have about 50,000 nuclear warheads. France, Great Britain, China, India, and Israel all have nuclear weapons for a total of more than 60,000 nuclear warheads.[9]

Here is what would happen if a 1-megaton bomb exploded in a populated area of the United States. While conventional bombs produce only one destructive effect—the shock wave—nuclear weapons produce many destructive effects. At the moment of explosion, when the temperature of the gasified weapon material reaches stellar levels, the pressure is millions of times the normal atmospheric pressure. At the same time, radiation (gamma rays, a high-energy form of electromagnetic radiation) flows into the environment, destroying whatever is in its path, killing all humans within a 6-mile radius (destroying or polluting most vegetation and animal life as well), so that the survivors could not eat anything in the area.

At the same time an electromagnetic pulse is generated by the intense gamma ray radiation. At a high altitude this can produce such a surge of voltage that it would cripple communications throughout the United States. If a bomb exploded in the stratosphere over the center of the country, it could generate an electromagnetic pulse strong enough to cripple the nation's electrical circuits and bring its economy to a screeching halt.

When the fusion and fission reactions of the bomb have taken place, a giant fireball takes shape. It expands, radiating harmful X-rays into the air in the form of a thermal pulse, a wave of blinding light and intense heat, which can cause second-degree burns in exposed humans in an area of 280 square miles (a 20-megaton bomb would do this over a 2460-square-mile area). The fires from the thermal blast will cause raging fires, which will destroy everything for miles around.

At the same time the total reaction of the explosion causes an enormous blast wave to be sent out in all directions. The blast wave of an air-burst 1-megaton bomb can flatten all but the strongest buildings within a radius of $4\frac{1}{2}$ miles (a 20-megaton bomb can destroy everything within a 12 mile radius).

As the fire ball burns, it rises, condensing water from the surrounding atmosphere to form the characteristic mushroom cloud. This mixture will return to earth as radioactive fallout, most of it in the form of fine ash. This fallout will be carried downwind for thousands of miles, exposing human beings to radiation disease, an illness that is fatal if intense enough.

One of the global effects of the detonation would be the partial destruction of the ozone layer in the stratosphere. The nitrogen oxides from the explosion would flow upward and cause chemical reactions that would result in the depletion of the ozone layer, which filters the sun's harmful ultraviolet rays. As much as 70 percent of the ozone layer could be destroyed, resulting in an epidemic of cancer.

Another effect would be the nuclear winter. The ashes and soot cast up from the explosions would cloud, thereby blocking, the sun's heat from the earth, causing a new Ice Age to ensue and killing most human life.

The effect of 300 1-megaton bombs on the United States would be the destruction of over 140 million people in a few days. Since 60 percent of the population lives in an area of 18,000 square miles, they could be annihilated with fewer than 300 bombs in a short time. Jack Geiger wrote[10]:

> The landscape would be strewn with millions of corpses of human beings and animals. This alone is a situation without precedent in history. There would be an immense source of pollution of water and food. If you read the literature concerning natural disasters such as floods and typhoons, you find that there is always an associated danger of cholera or typhoid. The corpses would also feed a fast-growing population of insects. . . . Naturally, medical measures to fight disease would not be taken, since the blast would have destroyed virtually all medical facilities."

The living might well envy the dead, for their lives would have little to look forward to. Strontium-90 (which resembles calcium in its chemical composition and so gets into milk products and then into humans through the milk) eventually causes bone cancer. Most animals, especially large ones like cattle, and most trees would die; lakes and rivers would be poisoned by radiation; and the affected soil would lose its nutrients and, consequently, its ability to produce food. "In sum, a full-scale nuclear attack on the United States would devastate the natural environment on a scale unknown since early geologic times, when, in response to natural catastrophes . . . sudden mass extinctions of species and whole ecosystems occurred all over the earth."[11] What would survive? Mainly grass and small insects. The United States would become a republic of insects and grass.

A nuclear war violates the principles of a Just War. It violates principles 4 (aiming at bringing about peace in which the enemy is respected), 5 (proportionality), and 6 (discrimination between combatants and noncombatants). This is why the Roman Catholic Bishops have declared that using nuclear weapons is inherently immoral.

Utilitarians and contractualists also generally condemn nuclear war. The short-term and long-term destruction of such a war would be so terrible that it defies the power of words to describe. However, these theories might justify selective use of nuclear weapons, as theorists from both of these camps justify the use of the atomic bomb on Hiroshima and Nagasaki to bring Japan to surrender and thus save hundreds of thousands of lives. For utilitarians the principle of the Lesser Evil applied. Do whatever will minimize evil! For contractualists the bombing was an instrument of enlightened self-interest.

But both utilitarians and contractualists agree that we must prevent a nuclear war. In the shadow of a nuclear holocaust the deontologic, utilitarian, and contractualist tend to converge, as do abolitionist and realist positions. Such an act of madness violates Just War principles, it violates the principle of utility, and it is not in anyone's interest. The threat of nuclear war provides a powerful incentive for all people throughout the earth to learn to live together in peace.

CONCLUSION

War has typically been a sacrament of state, a holy rite of passage for young males, bringing out the virtues of courage, discipline, devotion, decisiveness, and endurance, as well as engendering the thrill of strenuous competition as no other activity on the face of the earth. The horror is the thrill. Now, however, given the threat of a nuclear holocaust, we can no longer afford to play that game, except arguably where nuclear weapons are excluded, although even here the sport becomes increasingly stupid. As the globe shrinks and the powers of destruction grow, we need to use more rational means for the resolution of conflicts of interest.

Nevertheless, the high virtues and heightened tension of mortal powers recognized in war deserve recognition and an outlet. Other institutions must substitute for war, giving pride of place to valor, devotion, creative intelligence, endurance, and the thrill of difficult accomplishment. This is my reason for tolerating sports like football and hockey, which are otherwise crude and dangerous. They may be, in the words of William James, the "moral equivalent of war." Humans beings, at least at this stage of evolution, need the challenge of great heights, of physical endurance, of great causes to which to devote themselves. On to

Mt. Everest, the football field, the Peace Corps, the Environmental Protection Program, the Space Program, sacrificial service in the poorest, most dangerous, quarters of the globe, but away from war! A Peace Army into which every young person would be conscripted for 2 years to serve human need instead of human destruction should eventually replace present practices of war armies.

Economic boycotts and international censure must replace armed conflict, and arms sales to belligerent nations must be curtailed. Eventually, nation states will probably have to relinquish some sovereignty to the United Nations, which is the only agency at present able to adjudicate international conflicts of interest. Ensuring its impartiality and moral integrity, and increasing its power to act against aggression without itself becoming despotic, are two of the great challenges facing our generation.

Finally, we should reject both philosophies adumbrated at the beginning of this chapter—the idea that nothing is worth dying for and the idea that war is an acceptable way of attaining glory. Men and women must learn to love the dove as we have hitherto loved the hawk!

Study Questions

1. Discuss the three major philosophies of war. What are the strengths and weaknesses of each?

2. Discuss pacifism. Is it a deeply moral position or, as Jan Narveson argues, a fundamentally incoherent position?

3. What is the Just War theory? What are its principles? Distinguish between "jus ad bellum" and "jus in bello." Do these principles apply to modern warfare? Would adhering to these principles handicap one side against a ruthless enemy who stopped at nothing in order to prevail?

4. Is there a clear distinction between compatants and noncombatants as posited by Just War theory? Or are all who contribute to the enemy's effort in any way to be viewed as legitimate targets of aggression?

5. What should be our policy toward nuclear weapons? Should we work for universal nuclear disarmament or maintain nuclear weapons as a credible deterrent?

Endnotes

1. William James, " The Moral Equivalent of War," *The Writings of William James,* John J. McDermott, ed. (New York: Random House, 1967), p. 661.
2. Dionysius of Halicarnassus, *On Thucydides,* W. Kendrick Pritchell, trans., quoted in Michael Walzer, *Just and Unjust Wars* (New York: Harper & Row, 1977), p. 6.

3. Tertullian, quoted in George Forell, *History of Christian Ethics* (Philadelphia: Fortress Press, 1972), p. 123.

4. Helmut von Moltke, quoted in Arnold Toynbee, *War and Civilization*, Oxford: Oxford University Press, 1950), p. 16.

5. Quoted in Toynbee, Ibid, p. 16.

6. I am indebted for this argument to Jan Narveson's article "Pacifism: A Philosophical Analysis," in Richard Wasserstrom's anthology *War and Morality* (Belmont: Wadsworth, 1970).

7. Richard Wasserstrom, "On the Morality of War: A Preliminary Inquiry," in *War and Morality*, Richard Wasserstrom, ed. (Belmont, Calif.: Wadsworth, 1970).

8. Address to the Nation by President Harry S. Truman, August 9, 1945, quoted in Robert Tucker, *The Just War* (1960), pp. 21f.

9. I am indebted to the account given by Jonathan Schell in his brilliant work, *The Fate of the Earth* (New York: Alfred Knopf, 1982), Chapter I, for my account of the destructiveness of nuclear weapons

10. Ibid, p. 68.

11. Ibid, p. 64.

World Hunger

—UNITED NATIONS DECLARATION ON HUMAN RIGHTS, 1948

*Feeding the hungry in some countries only keeps them alive longer
to produce more hungry bellies and disease and death.*

—JOSEPH FLETCHER, "GIVE IF IT HELPS BUT NOT IF IT HURTS"

More than one third of the world goes to bed hungry each night. Ten
thousand people starve to death each day. Another two billion are
malnourished. The United Nations Food and Agriculture Organization
estimates that 460 million people are permanently hungry, almost half
of these being children. While famines have raged through parts of
Africa and Asia, another third of the world, the industrialized West, lives
in relative affluence, wasting food or overeating. The rich get richer and
the poor poorer.

World hunger is one of the most intractable problems that face
humankind today. What can be done about it? What obligations, if any,
do we in the affluent West have to distant, needy people, those who
hunger or are starving? To what extent should population policies be
tied to hunger relief? These are the questions discussed in this chapter.

I will discuss three responses to these questions: (1) the Neo-
Malthusian response set forth by Garret Hardin; (2) the Conservative
(or Libertarian) response represented by Thomas Hobbes, Robert
Nozick, and others; and (3) the Liberal response, exemplified by Peter
Singer and Richard Watson. After this I will suggest alternative positions, taking into consideration the valid insights of each of these other
positions.

THREE ETHICAL THEORIES AND
THEIR RESPONSES TO WORLD HUNGER

The contrast between Neo-Malthusians and Liberals can hardly be imagined to be greater. Liberals assert that we have a duty to feed the hungry in famine-ridden areas because the hungry have a right to it or because of utilitarian reasons maximizing welfare or happiness. Neo-Malthusians assert that we have an opposite duty to refrain from feeding the hungry in famine-ridden areas for utilitarian reasons. Conservatives take the middle road in this debate and assert that while we do not have a duty to feed the hungry, it is permissible and praiseworthy to do so. It is an act of supererogation, an act going beyond the call of duty. We begin with the Neo-Malthusians.

Neo-Malthusianism

The Reverend Thomas Robert Malthus (1766–1834) was an English clergyman who set forth the theory that population size tends to outrun food production, leading to misery until war, disease, famine, and other disasters restore a natural balance. Partly owing to modern agriculture technology and the spread of birth control devices, Malthus's predictions haven't been universally fulfilled. In the United States and Canada, for example, food production has been substantially above what is needed for their population. Neo-Malthusians are those ecologists who accept Malthus's basic thesis but modify it in the light of technologic innovation. A nation that is not holding the proper food:population ratio should not be helped from the outside by increments of food. To feed such sick societies is, to quote Alan Gregg, a former vice president of the Rockefeller Foundation, like feeding a cancer. "Cancerous growths demand food; but, as far as I know, they have never been cured by getting it."[1]

The most prominent Neo-Malthusian today is Garrett Hardin, Emeritus Professor of Human Biology at the University of California at Santa Barbara, who in a series of articles set forth the idea of Lifeboat Ethics.[2] Hardin's position can be succinctly stated through three metaphors he has made famous: "lifeboat," "tragedy of the commons," and "the ratchet." Let us examine his use of each of these.

1. Lifeboat.   The world is compared to a sea in which a few lifeboats (the affluent nations) are surrounded by hordes of drowning people (the populations of the poor nations). Each lifeboat has a limited carrying capacity, which is such that it cannot possibly take on more than a tiny fraction of the drowning without jeopardizing the lives of its passengers. Besides, need of a safety factor always dictates that we ought to leave a healthy margin between the actual number on board and the possible number. The optimum population is somewhat below the maximum population. According to Hardin the affluent nations are, at present, right around that optimum figure, probably beyond it, so that it is self-destructive to take on the world's poor. Not only must we adhere to a population policy of zero-growth, but we must have stringent immigration policies that prevent immigrants from swamping our boat.

2. The "Tragedy of the Commons."   Imagine a public field (a "commons") where shepherds have been grazing their sheep for centuries. Because of the richness of the field and the poverty of the shepherds, the field is never overgrazed. Now there comes a time when the carrying capacity of the field is reaching its limit. At this point it is in the short-term rational self-interest of each farmer to add to the field in spite of its limitations. The prudential farmer reasons that by grazing yet one more sheep he will be reaping a positive factor of 1 (the value brought on by the extra sheep) and losing only a fraction of the negative unit 1, the loss of the field's resources, since all the herdsmen share that equally whether they participate in overgrazing or not. So it is in each shepherd's interest to overgraze. But if too many shepherds act in their short-term self-interest in this way, it soon will be against their interest, for the pasture will be ruined. Hence the tragedy of the commons! A similar tragedy is occurring in our use of natural resources. We are in danger of depleting the world's resources through wanton overuse. To prevent such a tragedy we must have mutually agreed upon, mutually coercive laws, laws against population increase, overgrazing, overfishing, deforestation, pollution, and the like. Each nation must manage its own commons, and where one fails to do so, it must be left to its own misery. Benevolent intervention on the part of misguided do-gooders is likely only to increase the misery. But this leads to the next metaphor.

3. The Ratchet.   Hardin argues that there is a natural relationship in ecosystems so that once a species has overshot the carrying capacity of the environment, nature takes care of the situation by causing a die-back of the population of the species and eventually restores a balance (Fig. 10–1). For example, when there is a serious decline in the natural predators of deer in an area, the deer population tends to increase exponentially until it overshoots the carrying capacity of the land for deer. The land cannot provide for this increase of deer, so they begin to starve, causing a die-back in their population, until conditions are such that they can increase at a normal pace. Likewise with human population systems. Once people in a given area have exceeded the carrying capacity of the environment, there will come a period of scarcity, resulting, à la Malthus, in famine, disease, and war over scarce resources, which results

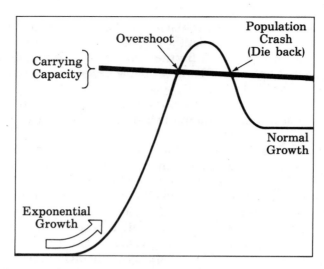

FIGURE 10 –1   *The relation of the carrying capacity of an environment to exponential population growth.*

in a die-back or lowering of the population below the level of the carrying capacity. Nature will take care of the tragedy of the commons. When people refuse to constrain their procreative instincts, nature intervenes and does it for them.

Now let some well-meaning altruists intervene to thwart nature's iron law. The altruists send food to the starving and fend off the famine for a time. But what happens? The people procreate and the population increases even further beyond the carrying capacity of the land, so that soon even more people are starving, so that another even greater altruistic effort is needed to stave off the worsening situation. And so a herculean effort is accomplished, and the population is saved once again. But where does this process lead? Only to an eventually disaster. The ratchet effect keeps raising the level of the population without coming to terms with the natural relation of the population to its environment, and that is where Malthus's law is valid (Fig. 10–2). Sending food to those who are not taking voluntary steps to curb their population size is like feeding a cancer.

For Hardin it is wrong to give aid to those who are starving in overpopulated countries because of the ratchet effect. It only causes more misery in the long run. "How can we help a foreign country to escape overpopulation? Clearly the worst thing we can do is send food. . . . Atomic bombs would be kinder. For a few moments the misery would be acute, but it would soon come to an end for most of the people, leaving a very few survivors to suffer thereafter."[3]

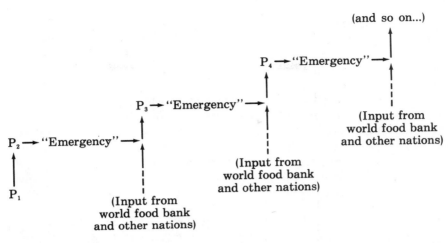

FIGURE 10 –2   *The ratchet effect.*

Furthermore, we have a natural duty to our children and to posterity to maintain the health of the planet as a whole. By using resources now in this short-term fix we rob our children and future generations of their rightful inheritance. The claims of future people in this case override those of distant people.

In summary, Hardin has three arguments against giving aid to the poor in distant lands: (1) It will threaten our lifeboat by affecting the safety factor and causing our carrying capacity to become strained; (2) It will only increase the misery due to the ratchet effect; and (3) It will threaten the welfare of our descendants to whom we have prior obligations. For all these reasons we are morally required not to give aid to the hungry.

What can be said about this kind of reasoning? Is Hardin right about the world's situation? Let us examine the arguments more closely. Consider (1), the lifeboat argument. Is the metaphor itself appropriate? Are we really so nicely separate from the poor of the world? Or is the truth that we are vitally interdependent, profiting from the same conditions that contribute to the misery of the underdeveloped nations? Haven't colonialization and commercial arrangements worked out to increase the disparity between the rich and the poor nations of the earth? We extract cheap raw materials from poor nations and sell these nations expensive manufactured goods (for example, radios, cars, computers and weapons) instead of appropriate agricultural goods and training. The structure of tariffs and internal subsidies discriminates selectively against underdeveloped nations. Multinational corporations place strong inducements on these countries to produce cash crops such as coffee and cocoa instead of food crops. Besides this, the United States and other Western nations have often used aid to bolster dictatorships like the Somoza regime in Nicaragua and the military juntas in Chile and El Salvador, which have resisted social change that would have redistributed wealth more equitably. For example, in 1973 when President Allende of Chile requested aid from the United States, not only was he turned down but our government aided in bringing his reformist government to ruin. When the military junta that replaced Allende took power and promised to maintain American business interests, eight times the amount of aid Allende had asked for was given to that government.

Hardin's lifeboat metaphor grimly obscures the fact that we have profited and are profiting from the economic conditions in the Third World. Perhaps a more apt metaphor than "lifeboat" might be a powerful multinational corporation octopus with tentacles clutching weapons and reaching out into diverse regions of the globe. Our nation protects, encourages, and even intervenes in the affairs of other nations on the basis of its relations with these corporations. But if that is the case, how can we dissociate ourselves from the plight of these countries? Keeping the poor out of our lifeboats might be permissible if we hadn't built the boats out of rubber taken from them in the first place. The fact is, even if you can justify the commercial dealings we have with the rest of the world, we are already involved with the hungry of the world in a way that the lifeboat metaphor belies.

The question of justice haunts Hardin's argument. He admits that ofttimes survival policies are unjust, but he argues that survival overrides justice, that it is better to survive unjustly than to be just and let everyone perish. "Complete injustice, complete catastrophe." But this is to fail to consider a whole middle range of possibilities where justice would be at least a contributing factor in the solution, which would take the need for one's own survival into consideration. Justice would demand some attention to redistributing the wealth of the world. At present the United States, with less than 6 percent of the world's population, consumes some 35 percent of its food (much of it thrown into garbage cans or rotting in storage silos) and 38 percent of its energy and is responsible for creating 33 percent of the world's pollution. If Hardin is so concerned about preserving the world's purity and resources for posterity, justice would require that we sacrifice the overfed, overweight, overnourished, greedy Americans who throw into garbage cans more food than some nations eat.

Regarding the carrying capacity and ratchet effect, several objections are in order. First of all, how does Hardin know which nations have exceeded their carrying capacity? The very notion of the carrying capacity, given our technologic ability to produce new varieties of food, is a flexible one. Perhaps experts can identify some regions of the earth (for example, deserts) where the land can sustain only a few people, but one ought to be cautious in pronouncing that Bangladesh or India or some country in Africa is in that state. Too many variables abound. New agricultural or fishing techniques or cultural practices may offset the validity of technical assessments.

Secondly, Hardin is too dogmatic in proclaiming the law-like dictum that to give aid to the poor is to cause the escalation of misery. Granted, we can make things worse by merely giving food handouts, and population policy is needed to prevent the ratchet effect that Hardin rightly warns against. But there are intelligent ways to aid, such as giving agricultural instruction and technologic know-how to nations committed to responsible population policies; offering food in emergencies with encouragement to eradicate those conditions that cause famine and malnutrition; being a good example of what a just, disciplined, frugal society should be. But to dismiss these options out of hand and simply advocate pushing people off our lifeboat is as oversimplistic as it is cruel.

Finally, Hardin's food–population theory ignores the growing evidence that, contrary to the ratchet projections, population growths are affected by many complex conditions other than food. Specifically, a number of socioeconomic conditions can be identified that cause parents to have fewer offspring. Birth rates can fall quite rapidly, sometimes before modern birth control devices are available. These conditions include parental security and faith in the future, the improved status of women in the society, literacy, and lower infant mortality. Procuring these conditions requires agricultural reform, some redistribution of wealth, increased income and employment, better health services, and fresh expenditures on education. Evidence suggests that people who perceive the benefits of a smaller family will act prudently. The theory that favorable socioeconomic conditions will cause people to bring down their birth rate is called "The Benign Demographic Transition Theory." Separate studies by Revelle, Rich, Eberstadt, and Brown have shown that several countries that have progressed in these areas have cut their birth rate dramatically.[4] China is the most successful nation in this regard, bringing its birth rate down from 40 per 1000 people to 30 in about 5 years' time. Cuba has brought its birth rate down to 27 per 1000. The Benign Demographic Transition theory still needs corroboration. It may not always work (for example, religious beliefs may militate against small families), but Hardin should take the evidence for it into consideration. For many of us, it is grounds for hope.

Liberalism

The Liberal position on world hunger is that we have a duty to help the poor in distant lands. There is something inherently evil about affluent people failing to come to the aid of the poor when they could do so without great sacrifice. Liberal theorists on this issue come in several varieties. Some are utilitarians who argue that sharing our abundance and feeding the poor will very likely maximize utility or happiness. Some are deontologists who argue that we have a fundamental duty to use our surplus to aid those less well off. Some deontologists simply find it self-evident that the needy have a right to our resources. Witness the Presidential Commission on World Hunger, "Whether one speaks of human rights or basic human needs, the right to food is the most basic of all. . . . The correct moral and ethical position on hunger is beyond debate."[5] Others appeal to the principle of justice, arguing that the notion of fairness requires that we aid the least best off in the world. Still others are radical egalitarians—perhaps the label "liberal" doesn't strictly apply to them—who argue that the principle of equality overrides even the need for survival so that we should redistribute our resources equitably even if it means that all of us will be malnourished and risk perishing. I think that we can capture most of what is vital to the liberal program if we examine Peter Singer's theory, which covers the first two types of liberalism, and Richard Watson's theory, which is a version of radical egalitarianism.

Peter Singer's article "Famine, Affluence, and Morality,"[6] written on the eve of the 1971 famine in Bangladesh, sets forth two principles, either of which would drastically alter our lifestyles and require us to provide substantial assistance to distant, poor and hungry people. The *Strong Principle* states that "if it is in our power to prevent something bad from happening without thereby sacrificing anything of *comparable* importance, we ought morally to do it." While this has similarities to utilitarian principles, it differs from them in that it does not require maximizing happiness, simply the amelioration of suffering through sacrifice of our goods to the point where we are just about at the same place as the sufferer. The idea behind this principle is utilitarian: diminishing marginal utility, which states that transferring goods from those with surplus to those with needs generally increases total utility. For example, if you have $100 for your daily food allowance and I have no allowance at all, your giving me some of your money will actually increase the good that the money accomplishes, for the gain of, say, $10 by me will enable me to survive, thus outweighing the loss you suffer. But there will come a point where giving me that extra dollar will not make a difference to the total good. At that point you should stop giving. If we were to follow Singer's strong principle, we would probably be giving a vast proportion of our GNP (gross national product) to nonmilitary foreign aid instead of the present 0.21 percent (that's two tenths of one per cent), or the 0.7 percent advocated by the United Nations for rich countries.

Singer's *Weak Principle* states that we ought to act to prevent bad things from happening if doing so will not result in our sacrificing anything *morally significant.* He asks you to suppose that you are walking past a shallow pond and see a child drowning. You can save the child with no greater inconvenience than wading into the water and muddying your suit or dress. Should you not jump into the pond and rescue the child? Singer thinks it is self-evident that nothing morally significant is at stake in the sacrifice.

While Singer prefers the Strong Principle, he argues that the Weak Principle is sufficient to ground our duty to aid needy, distant people, for what difference does it make if the drowning child is in your home town or in Africa or Asia? "It makes no moral difference whether the person I can help is a neighbor's child 10 yards away or a Bengali whose name I shall never know, 10,000 miles away." He or she is still a human being and the same minimal sacrifice is required. Furthermore, the principle makes no distinction between cases in which I am the only person who can do anything and cases in which I am just one among many who can help. I have a duty in either case to see that what is needed is accomplished. Call this the "No Exception Proviso."

Singer's two principles have generated considerable debate and many ethicists have accepted one or both of them, but each has problems. John Arthur has noted in his critique of Singer that the Strong Principle is too strong and the Weak Principle is too weak.[7] On the Strong Principle our right to our property and lifestyles are too easily overridden by the needs of others. For example, if I meet a stranger going blind and prevent her being completely blind by giving her one of my eyes, I should take steps to have my eye removed—even, according to the No Exception Proviso, if there are others on whom she has a greater claim to some assistance than she has on me. Likewise, if I meet a man about to lose his kidneys or lungs, I have a prima facie duty to give him one of my kidneys or lungs, a duty that can be overridden only by finding someone on whom he has a stronger claim who will donate his or her organ. Woe the person who meets someone in need of all three of these organs—an eye, a lung, a kidney! If no one else is doing his or her duty, you are left with the responsibility of yielding your organs—even if this results, as it surely will, in a severe change in your lifestyle. So long as you have not reduced your lot to the level of the other person's, you must go on sacrificing—even for strangers.

Richard Watson's position[8] is even more severe than Singers. From a deontologic perspective he argues that the principle of equal worth of individuals calls for the food of the world being distributed equally. "All human beings are moral equals with equal rights to the necessities of life. Differential treatment of human beings thus should be based only on their freely chosen actions and not on accidents of their birth and environment." It is our sacred duty to share scarce resources with every needy person even if this means that we all will be malnourished, even if no one would get sufficient food, so that everyone perished. Equality trumps survival, even the survival of the human race.

Singer's Strong Principle and Watson's Equality-Absolute are not valid moral principles. An adequate moral theory must make room for self-regarding reasons. I am required to make *reasonable* sacrifices for others, but not at the cost of what would severely detract from the quality of my own life. Watson explicitly rejects the notion of reasonableness in morality. Morality is often unreasonable, according to him. But I see no reason to accept that verdict. If morality were truly unreasonable, rational people would be advised to opt out of it and choose a more rational Quasi-Morality in its place. My thesis throughout this book is that moral principles are reasonable requirements. In general they are in our long-term interest.

Of course, you are free to go beyond the call of duty and donate your organs to strangers. It is certainly noble of you to volunteer to do so. But such supererogatory acts are not duties as such. Extreme utilitarians and absolutist egalitarians confuse morality with extreme altruism or saintliness.

We turn to Singer's Weaker Principle. If we can prevent an evil by sacrificing something not morally significant, we should do so. This seems closer to the truth, but John Arthur has argued that it is too weak, for what can be morally significant varies from person to person. For example, my record collection or collection of rare pieces of art might be a significant part of what makes life worth living for me, so that to sacrifice them for the poor would be of moral significance. Is giving up owning a television or having a nice car or having a nice wardrobe morally significant? For many people they are. Nevertheless, there are occasions in which sacrificing these things for the poor or needy might be morally required of me. Even in the case of a child drowning in the pond, you could refuse to jump in the water to save the child, using Singer's Weak Principle, for you could argue that having clean, unspoilt clothes is morally significant for you. Of course, it would really have to be the case that they were morally significant, but for many they are.

Of course, Singer could respond that Arthur's objection fails because he is overly relativizing morally significant to the individual. There is an objective truth to the matter of whether something really is morally significant. He would need to qualify his principle of what is morally significant by relational terms: In situation S object O is morally significant to person P (whether he or she realizes it or not). Compared with saving someone's life, wearing clean, unspoilt clothes really is not morally significant whatever the misguided dandy might think to the contrary. Not every supposed morally significant trait is really so. If I believe that burning witches is the way to save our nation from the devil and go around burning those who fit my description, I am simply misguided. Likewise, if I think that my baseball card collection is more important than saving my best friend's life, I have a bad set of priorities— friends really are more valuable than baseball cards and if I fail to realize this, I am missing a deep moral truth.

While Singer's Weak Principle, suitably qualified, can survive the kind of attack that philosophers like Arthur hurl at it, it may not be good enough to get him the hunger relief that he is advocating. Other factors must also be addressed. For example, do needy strangers have rightful claims on my assets even though I have done nothing to cause their sorry state? Do the starving have rights to my property? We turn to the Conservative Position, which answers these questions in the negative.

Conservativism

Conservatives on world hunger argue that we have no duty at all to give aid to distant needy people. Representative of the view in question are such Libertarians as John Hospers, Robert Nozick, and Ayn Rand, and Contractualists like Thomas Hobbes and, more recently, Gilbert Harman, Howard Kahane, and William Nelson.[9] Typically, conservatives, in the minimalist sense I am using the term, reject the notion that we have positive rights that entail duties on the part of others to come to our aid or promote our good unless there is a contractual agreement between us. The one right we have is that of freedom: the right not to be interfered with, the right to possess our property in peace. So long as I have a legitimate claim on my property (that is, I have not acquired it through fraud or coercion) no one may take it from me, and I may refuse to share it regardless of how needy others are.

We may not positively harm others, but we need not help them either. No moral duty obligates you to dirty your clothes by trying to save the child drowning in the muddy pond. Of course, it shows bad character not to save the child, and we should endeavor to be charitable with our surplus and support good causes, but these are not strictly moral duties, but optional ideals. So it follows that if hungry Esau is prompted to sell his birthright to that feisty chef Jacob, so much the worse for Esau; and if a poor African country decides to contract with a Western corporation to shift from growing a high-protein crop to a cash crop like coffee, so long as no external force was used in the agreement, the contract is entirely just, and the corporation need feel no guilt when the poor nation undergoes a famine and finds itself unable to supply its people with adequate protein. No rights have been violated. The country simply made a foolish choice.

If you believe that the contractual approach to ethics, which we examined in Chapter 1, is the correct approach, the conservative position will appeal to you. It may be the best approach, all things considered, but there are certain weaknesses you should be aware of. Conservative contractualism tends to be too narrow in its sympathies. Morality, in large part, has to do with the promotion of human flourishing and ameliorating suffering, as I have suggested in the Chapter 1, so that we seem to have some duties to help others. On the contractualist model the 39 people who for 45 minutes watched Kitty Genovese get beaten to death, who did not lift a finger to call the police or lift their windows to shout at the assailant, did nothing wrong. But if we have a duty to promote human flourishing and ameliorate suffering, these onlookers did have a duty to do something on Ms. Genovese's behalf, and they are to be faulted for not coming to her aid.

It would seem, then, that there are positive duties as well as negative ones. Whether under a utilitarian or deontologic framework, we have obligations to ameliorate suffering and promote human flourishing. To what extent we should do these things and under what conditions are more difficult questions.

There is a moderate position between the liberal and the conservative that accepts part of each position but rejects other parts. It goes as follows. Morality originates in group living, tribes. People discover that certain rules are necessary for survival and happiness: rules against killing each other, against breaking promises, against violating property rights, against lying and cheating, and rules promoting justice, cooperation, respect for others, and beneficence. Those living in a society implicitly agree to live by this "core morality." They resolve their conflicts of interest through compromise or impartial third bodies—the primitive origins of law. But they notice that there are other groups that do not respect their lives or property, and there is no way to resolve differences through impartial review. The Other is the enemy toward whom the rules do not apply. Indeed, it is only by not respecting the enemy's life and property that one can survive and flourish.

Eventually, the two groups learn to accept an intertribal core morality. They begin with a mutual nonaggression pact, respect each other as equals, cooperate instead of fight with each other, and subject their differences to an impartial review. So two tribes acknowledge a similar core morality and apply it between them. Nevertheless, in many situations, members of a tribe will feel a greater responsibility to aid members of their own family and tribe rather than members of the neighboring one. If my child, a neighboring child, and a child of another tribe all need a pair of shoes, and I have only enough resources to procure one pair, I will feel a duty to give them to my child. If I can procure two pair easily, I will give the first pair to my child, but sell the second pair at a low price to my neighbor. If I go into the shoe-making business, I will still be likely to give favored treatment to my neighbor over the person from the neighboring tribe. Greater opportunity for reciprocity arises with my neighbor than with the family of the neighboring tribe, so it makes sense to treat that family special.

Moderate moral theory recognizes special responsibilities to family, friends, and neighbors. This is why Singer's drowning child example is misleading. I can only do so much good. I can only save so many drowning children. While I may have a duty to give of my surplus to help save drowning children in a distant land, I have a stronger duty to help those with whom I have intimate or contractual ties.

This said, the other side of the coin needs to be looked at and the liberal program acknowledged. Another aspect of morality is the enlargement of the circle of benevolence and flourishing, the utilitarian aspect of maximizing good. We need to expand the small circle of moral consideration and commitment from family, community, and country to include the whole world. We need to do this for two reasons. First, it just is good to do so. Helping as many people (and animals) as possible without harming yourself is part of the meaning of the idea of promoting the flourishing of sentient beings. Second, it is in our self-interest to do so. Unless we learn to live together on this small planet, we may all perish. Humanity is no longer innocent. Technology is available to destroy all sentient life—atomic weapons, poisonous chemicals, and so forth. One nation's adverse environmental impact can affect the rest of the world. If one nation pollutes the air through spreading sulfur dioxide or carbon dioxide, the rest of the world suffers the effects. If the Brazilian or Peruvian farmers cut down large segments of the Amazon Rain Forest, we all receive less oxygen in the atmosphere. We are all in each other's debt. If we don't hang together, we *hang* alone.

So the same considerations that led to mutual cooperation between our original tribes must inform our global policies. A rational core morality must reign internationally. While we will still have priority commitments to family and friends, we cannot allow selfishness to hinder generous dealings with the rest of the world. So Hardin's metaphor of nations as lifeboats has only limited applicability. It may justify careful immigration policies that prevent overcrowding, but it should not prevent assistance to other nations who may be helped and who someday may be able to help us. In a sense the whole earth is just one great lifeboat in which we'll sink or float together.

But something must be said in Hardin's behalf. He points to a crucial problem that deserves our concentrated attention: population policy. Even if we finally opt for the benign demographic transition theory, many situations may not wait for that policy to take effect. The facts are that the population of the world is multiplying at an exponential rate. Since 1930 the earth's population has increased from 2 billion to the present 5.3 billion, heading for 6 billion by the year 2002 (Fig.10–3). In 1968 Paul and Anne Ehrlich wrote *Population Bomb*, warning that the population of the world (then 3.5 billion) was growing exponentially at a rate of 70 million per year and that if strong measures were not taken, we would likely have Malthusian problems of famine and disease. Critics pejoratively labeled such cautioners as "Doomsdayers," but they have been proved correct.

Crowded conditions prevail in many parts of the world. Famines have become worse in areas of Africa. Today the global population is growing not by 70 million per year, but by 95 million. The growth rate is 1.8 percent, which means the earth's population is likely to double in 39 years, so that it will be 10.6 billion by 2030, doubling again by 2069 to 21.6 billion, unless there is a die-back—or policies of population control are implemented. The present growth rate in Guatemala, Honduras, Nicaragua, Ecuador, the Philippines, Bangladesh, Ghana,

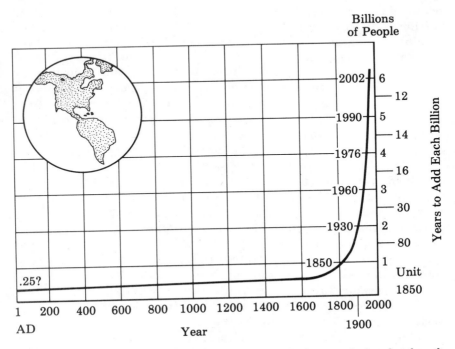

FIGURE 10–3   *J curve of the world's population growth (future projections based on the present growth rate of 1.7 percent).*

Botswana, Zimbabwe, Morocco, Malawi, and Thailand is 3.3 percent per annum, which means a doubling in about 21 years. Jordan and Syria's rate is 3.8 percent, while Kenya's 4.2 percent, a doubling time of 17 years. A slight increase in the growth rate would result in the world's population density becoming that of present-day New York City by the year 2300. Add to this the following: The innovative technologic development of food has leveled off, topsoil is being depleted, pesticide-resistant strains of crop destroyers are appearing throughout the earth's agricultural areas, and there is evidence of changing weather patterns, probably brought on by the Greenhouse Effect, causing diminished farm production.[10]

We have cause for alarm, and if the shouts of environmentalists like Hardin are needed to wake us up, let us thank him for waking us up—even as we work for kinder, more just solutions to the problem. The point is that hard choices have to be made, and food aid should be tied to responsible population control for the survival and well-being of humanity.

A proposal that improves on Hardin's Lifeboat Ethics is the Triage approach first set forth by Paul and William Paddock in *Famine—1975* and advocated by Joseph Fletcher.[11] The term *triage* (French for "sorting") comes from wartime medical policies. With a scarcity of physicians and resources to cope with battle casualties, the wounded were divided into three groups: those who would probably survive without medical treatment, those who would not survive even with treatment, and those for whom treatment would make the decisive difference. Only this last group would receive medical aid. The Paddocks and Fletcher urge us to apply the same policy to world hunger. Given limited ability and scarce resources to help, we should not aid those nations that will survive without our aid or those that will not be able to sustain themselves even with our help. We should direct all our attention to those nations for whom our input could make a decisive difference. The aim should be to enable these nations to become self-sufficient, responsive to the carrying capacity of their environment. As a Chinese proverb says, "Give a man a fish today and he will eat it for a day. Teach him how to fish, and he will eat for the rest of his days."

As repulsive as the triage strategy may be to many of us, it should not be dismissed out of hand. Perhaps at present no nation is hopeless, so that we still have time to forestall the nefarious effects of overpopulation. We should give the benign demographic theory a chance to work, supporting social reform at home and abroad with our actions and our pocketbook, but if we cannot effect global changes, the time for triage may soon be upon us. The Doomsdayers are to be taken seriously. They may not be correct, but their warnings should be heeded.

Meanwhile, moral wisdom mandates contributing personally to hunger relief organizations and urging national policy to providing agricultural know-how and technology to nations in dire need. At the same time we should support family planning programs both here and abroad, working to arrest the trend toward overpopulation, and aiming to provide each human being with as high a quality of life as is possible. The option is not food *or* population control, but food *and* population control. The world must see these as two sides of the same coin, a coin that is our entrance payment to a better future for all people.

If preceding discussion is correct, we do have a duty to give aid to the needy, both in our own country and in other lands. It is a duty to exercise benevolence to ameliorate suffering and promote human flourishing. We do not have a duty to reduce our lot to an equal poverty, as Watson and Singer's Strong Principle advocates, but we should be giving more than most of us are. No one can tell another person just how much he or she should be donating, but each of us must consult our consciences. Besides that we should be living as examples of ecologic responsibility, as good stewards of the earth's resources, and we should call upon our leaders to increase nonmilitary aid to underdeveloped countries where the need is greatest.

Study Questions

1. Discuss Thomas Malthus's views on the relationship between population and food production. Where was Malthus mistaken? What is the position of Neo-Malthusians like Garrett Hardin? Examine and evaluate Hardin's three arguments against giving aid to starving people of other countries.

2. What is the "Benign Demographic Transition Theory"? How strong is it and what might be said against its use in policy development?

3. Examine Peter Singer's arguments in favor of helping famine victims. Evaluate his principle "If it is in our power to prevent something bad from happening, without sacrificing anything else of comparable moral importance, we ought morally to do it." If we followed this principle, what would be the likely results? What moral considerations would outweigh our obligation to give aid to famine victims or anyone else in need?

4. How would a contractualist deal with the problem of aiding famine victims?

5. Discuss the notion of triage. How does it apply to the problem of world hunger?

Endnotes

1. Alan Gregg, "A Medical Aspect of the Population Problem," *Science* 121 (1955).

2. Garrett Hardin, "Lifeboat Ethics: The Case Against Helping the Poor," *Psychology Today* (1974); "Living on a Lifeboat" *BioScience* (1974); *The Limits of Altruism* (Bloomington: Indiana University Press, 1977).

3. Garrett Hardin, "The Immorality of Being Softhearted," *Stanford Alumni Almanac* (January 1969).

4. See Roger Revelle, "The Ghost at the Feast," *Science* 186 (1974); W. Rich, "Smaller Families through Social and Economic Progress," *Overseas Development Council Monograph* #7, Washington D.C., 1973; Nick Eberstadt, "Myths of the Food Crisis," *New York Review of Books*, February 19, 1976; Lester Brown, *In the Human Interest* (New York: Norton, 1974), p. 119; *World Without Borders* (New York: Praeger, 1974), pp. 140f; and M. S. Teitelbaum, "Relevance of Demographic Transition Theory in Developing Countries," *Science* 188 (1975).

5. Presidential Commission of World Hunger, *Overcoming World Hunger: The Challenge Ahead* (Washington, D.C.: Government Printing Office, 1980).

6. Peter Singer, "Famine, Affluence and Morality," *Philosophy and Public Affairs* (1972).

7. John Arthur, "Rights and Duty to Bring Aid," in William Aiken and Hugh LaFollette, eds., *World Hunger and Moral Responsibility* (Englewood Cliffs, N.J.: Prentice-Hall, 1977).

8. Richard Watson, "Reason and Morality in a World of Limited Food," in Aiken and LaFollette, op. cit.

9. John Hospers, *Libertarianism* (Los Angeles: Nash, 1971); Robert Nozick, *Anarchy, State and Utopia* (New York: Basic Books, 1974); Thomas Hobbes, *Leviathan* (1651); Gilbert Harman, "Moral Relativism Defended," *Philosophical Review* (1975); Howard Kahane, "Making the World Safe for Reciprocity," in Joel Feinberg, ed., *Reason and Responsibility*. (Belmont, Calif.: Wadsworth, 1989); and William Nelson, *What's in it for Me?* (Oxford: Westview Press, 1991). Ayn Rand, *The Virtues of Selfishness* (New York: New American Library, 1964) also holds this position from an explicitly egoistic perspective.

10. Statistics are based on the *Population and Vital Statistics Report of the United Nation Statistical Office* and the *U.N. Demographic Yearbook* 1990. Information is available through the Population Reference Bureau, 777 14th St., N.W., Suite 800, Washington, D.C. 20005. See also the journal *Population and Environment*, especially vol. 12, 3 (Spring 1991).

11. Paul and William Paddoch, *Famine—1975* (Boston: Little Brown, 1968) and Joseph Fletcher, "Give if it Helps, Not if it Hurts" in Aiken and LaFollette, op. cit.

CHAPTER 11

What Is Death? The Crisis of Criteria

A woman in New York is beaten by a man until she is unconscious. She is put on a ventilator until physicians decide that she is irreversibly comatose. The ventilator is then detached, and she dies. Later in court the lawyer for the man accused of beating her to death argues that the doctors, not the accused, killed the woman. For had the doctors not removed the respirator, the woman would still be alive.

In Kansas a man on a ventilator was declared brain dead, but when he was transported across the border to be buried in his home state, Oklahoma, he was declared alive again, since the definitions of death in the two states differ.

In a famous case in Kentucky, *Grey v. Swayer* (1952), a court had to decide which of two individuals, a man and a woman, would inherit a large sum of money. The will stated that the person who survived the other would inherit the money. In an automobile accident both parties were killed, but while the man soon lost his pulse, the woman, who had been decapitated, continued to spurt blood for a short time after the accident. Physicians testified that "a body is not dead so long as there is a heartbeat and that may be evidenced by the gushing of blood in spurts."[1] The court ruled on the basis of this cardiovascular definition of death that the woman survived the man—even though she had been decapitated before he died.

On May 24, 1968, a worker in Virginia named Bruce Tucker fell, sustaining a severe head injury. When the ambulance delivered him to the emergency department of the Medical College of Virginia Hospital, he was found to be bleeding within his brain. He was put on a ventilator and an operation was performed to relieve the pressure on the brain. It was unsuccessful, and Tucker was described by the physician in charge as "mechanically alive . . . [his] prognosis for recovery is nil and death imminent."

At the same time a patient named Joseph Klett was in a ward waiting for a donor heart. When the electroencephalogram attached to Tucker showed a flat line, the doctors concluded that he was "brain dead." They operated and transplanted his heart to Klett. Tucker's kidneys were also removed for transplantation.

Although Tucker's wallet contained his brother's business card, including a phone number and address only 15 blocks away from the hospital, no attempt was made to contact him. William Tucker, the brother, brought suit against the doctors who performed the operation, but the doctors were exonerated in court, even though Virginia law defined death as total cessation of all bodily functions. William Tucker, disappointed with the verdict, exclaimed, "There's nothing they can say to make me believe they didn't kill [my brother]."[2]

When is someone dead? Until the mid-twentieth century this was seldom a serious question. If someone failed to have a pulse and stopped breathing, this clearly determined that he or she was dead. But in the middle of this century biomedical technology developed ways to keep the body alive almost indefinitely, causing us to reflect anew on the meaning of death. Moreover, this same technology can transplant organs from one patient to another, so that we need a definition of death to guide us when to remove the organs from the person declared dead.

Several physicians, philosophers, and medical ethicists, including Henry Beecher, Robert M. Veatch, Tristram Engelhardt Jr., and Roland Puccetti, have called for a redefinition of death in terms of brain functioning, "brain death." Others, like Paul Ramsey and Hans Jonas, have opposed this move.

WHAT IS DEATH?

Four definitions of death appear in the literature: (1) the departure of the soul from the body; (2) the irreversible loss of the flow of vital fluids or the irreversible cessation of cardiovascular pulmonary function; (3) whole brain death; and (4) neocortical brain death.

The Loss of Soul. The first major philosopher to hold that death occurred with the departure of the soul was Plato, but the view is found in the Orthodox Jewish and Christian traditions and in the writings of René Descartes (1596–1650), who believed that the soul resided in the pineal gland and left the body at death. The sign of the departure was the cessation of breathing. The Orthodox Jews say that a person is dead only when the last breath is drawn.[3] Note that the Hebrew word for spirit,

Ruach, is the same word used for breath, and the Greek word *pneuma* has the same double meaning.

There are problems with this view. First, it is difficult to know what the soul is, let alone whether we are endowed with one (or more). Second, neurologic science can explain much of human behavior by an appeal to brain functioning, so that the notion of a separate spiritual entity seems irrelevant. Third, if a soul is in us and if it only leaves us after we have breathed our last, medical technology can keep the soul in the body for scores of years after the brain has ceased to function and, as far as we can tell, all consciousness has long disappeared. Unless we are really convinced that God has revealed this doctrine to us, we should dismiss it as unsupported by the best evidence available.

The Cardiopulmonary View. When the heart and lungs stop functioning, the person is dead. This has been the traditional medical definition. *Black's Law Dictionary* puts it this way: "The cessation of life: the ceasing to exist; defined by physicians as a total stoppage of the circulation of the blood, and a cessation of the animal and vital functions consequent thereupon, such as respiration, pulsation, etc." In *Thomas v. Anderson* a California District Court in 1950 quoted *Black's* and added, "Death occurs precisely when life ceases and does not occur until the heart stops beating and respiration ends. Death is not a continuous event and is an event that takes place at a precise time."[4]

This standard definition is problematic in that it goes against the intuitions of many of us that irreversibly comatose patients like Karen Ann Quinlan or Nancy Cruzon are not alive at all. Bodily functioning alone does not constitute human life. We need to be sentient and self-conscious.

The Whole Brain View. As Roland Puccetti puts it, Where the brain goes, there the person goes.[5] In the same year that Bruce Tucker had his heart and kidneys removed, the Ad Hoc Committee of the Harvard Medical School under the chairmanship of Dr. Henry K. Beecher met to decide on criteria for declaring a person dead. The study was a response to the growing confusion over the uses of biomedical technology in being able to keep physical life going for an indefinite period of time after consciousness has been irretrievably lost. It also was a response to the desire to obtain organs from "donors" who were permanently comatose but whose organs were undamaged—because of the ability of technology to keep the vital fluids flowing.

The Committee came up with four criteria that together would enable the examiner to pronounce a person dead: (1) unreceptivity and unresponsivity (i.e., no awareness of externally applied stimuli); (2) no movement or breathing without the use of artificial mechanisms; (3) no reflexes; the pupil is fixed and dilated and will not respond to bright lights; (4) a flat electroencephalogram, which indicates that there is no cerebral activity. The test must be repeated at least 24 hours later to rule out rare false-positives (such as those caused by drugs or hypothermia—the body's having a temperature of less than 90° F).

The Harvard Committee's criteria have been widely accepted as a safe set, allowing medical practitioners to detach patients from artificial respirators and to transfer organs to needy recipients. Of thousands of patients tested no one has regained consciousness who has met the criteria.

But critics have objected that the Harvard criteria are too conservative. By its norms patients who are permanently comatose or in persistent vegetative states, like Karen Ann Quinlan and Nancy Cruzon, would be considered alive, since their lower brainstems continued to function. Indeed, people have been recorded as living as long as 37 years in this unconscious state. Since they are alive and can be fed intravenously, or via gastric feeding tubes, we have an obligation to continue to maintain them. The worry is that hospitals and nursing homes could turn into mausoleums for the comatose. So a fourth view of death has arisen.

Neocortical Brain Death. What is vital to human existence? Henry Beecher, head of the Harvard Ad Hoc Committee, says "consciousness." Henry Veatch, a prominent medical ethicist, says it is our capacity for social interaction, involving the power of thought, speech, and consciousness. These higher functions are located in the neocortex of the cerebrum or upper brain, so that when a sufficient part of this section of our brain is destroyed, the patient is dead. As Tristram Engelhardt Jr. says, "If the cerebrum is dead, the person is dead."[6] An electroencephalogram can determine when the cerebrum has ceased to function.

Beecher, Veatch, and Engelhardt see human death as the loss of what is significant for human life. Veatch defines death this way: "Death means a complete change in the status of a living entity characterized by the irreversible loss of those characters that are essentially significant to it."[7]

Where does the truth lie? To understand what is going on in this debate we should note the relevant physiologic and neurophysiologic aspects. The brain has three basic anatomic parts (Fig. 11–1): (1) the cerebrum, with its outer layer, the cortex; (2) the cerebellum; and (3) the brainstem, including the midbrain, pons, and medulla oblongata. While the cerebrum is the locus of thought, memory, and feelings, consciousness itself remains a mystery. Many believe it to result from complex interrelations between the brainstem and cortex. The brain is kept alive by blood carrying oxygen. If it is deprived of oxygen for more than a few minutes, it sustains permanent damage. After 4 or 5 minutes of deprivation, it usually dies.

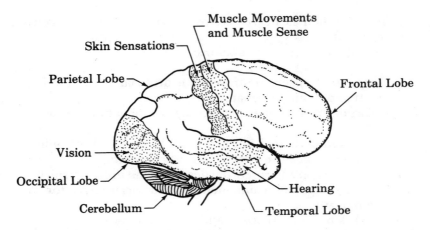

FIGURE 11–1   *The right cerebral hemisphere of man, seen from the side, showing the four lobes and the localized areas concerned with special functions. Association areas are unshaded. "Skin sensations" lie in the parietal lobe; "muscle movements," in the frontal lobe.*

Respiration, on the other hand, is controlled in the medulla of the brainstem (Fig. 11–2). When the medulla is destroyed, the body is unable to breath and normally dies, unless placed on an artificial respirator. When the respiratory system is destroyed, the heart is deprived of vital oxygen and dies. Unlike the respiratory system, the heart can pump blood without instructions from the brain, though the brain may control

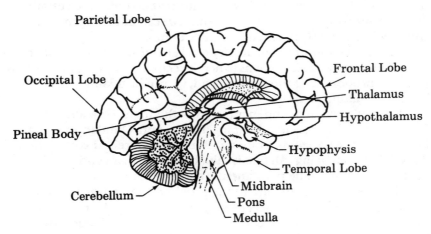

FIGURE 11–2   *The brain as seen in a vertical midline section.*

the heart rate. When the heart is destroyed, it cannot pump oxygen to the brain, so the brain dies.

We see the possible combinations:

1. Respiratory system destroyed but artificial respirator keeping heart and brain oxygenated.
2. Heart destroyed but artificial heart pumping blood to brain and lungs.
3. Cerebrum destroyed but heart and lungs still functioning (the persistent vegetative state). Neocortical death.
4. The brainstem and cerebrum destroyed but the heart still beating and the lungs still maintained by an artificial respirator. Whole brain death.
5. The brainstem, cerebrum, and heart all destroyed.

Biomedical technology has allowed these possibilities to arise. We are looking at the issue as a problem, but, in a sense, the problem is simply the downside of an enormous blessing. We should be grateful for such life-saving mechanisms. Without the ventilator many living people would be dead. Because of the ventilator we can keep organs fresh to transplant them to needy recipients.

Still the new wonders have brought with them new responsibilities and conceptual confusion about the meaning and nature of death.

The move to alter our definition of death is well motivated. First, we desire to alleviate the agony and financial burdens of relatives waiting for their comatose loved ones to die. How long must the relatives maintain irreversibly unconscious patients? Karen Ann Quinlan was kept alive in a nursing home for 10 years, and others have been maintained even longer. If we can agree to a view of death that includes the cessation of consciousness or neocortical functioning, we can mitigate the emotional suffering and financial hardship of loved ones.

Second, a redefinition of death would enable us to transplant organs from biologically viable humans to needy recipients. By keeping the body alive but pronouncing the person dead, we can justifiably transfer fresh organs to waiting patients.

There is a growing tendency to accept this logic. How absurd to care for bodies without minds! Keeping Karen Ann Quinlan in a nursing home for 10 years seems irrational. When the cerebral cortex dies, so does the human being. All that is valuable comes to an end with the end of conscious life. To be permanently comatose is to be dead.

However, this argument has a problem that must be addressed before its conclusion is accepted. The questionable move involves substituting a value for a fact or deriving a factual definition from our moral values. Veatch is guilty of this when he defines life as containing "those characteristics that are essentially significant to it" and death as the irreversible loss of those characteristics. The key phrase is "essentially significant," that is, *valuable.*

This redefinition muddies the waters. A comatose human whose lower brainstem is still functioning, whose heart is beating, and whose respiratory system is intact is still a living organism. Thus, something like the second view of death is correct. Death is an event, not a process, in which the biologic organism ceases to function. The vital fluids cease to flow and the heart and lungs cease forever.

David Mayo and Daniel Wikler make this point with regard to the dying process by distinguishing four possible states of the human organism.[8] Beginning with death proper the stages are:

Stage 4. All principal life systems of the organism (cardiovascular, central nervous, and pulmonary) irreversibly cease functioning. The organism as a whole permanently ceases to function. This is death proper.

Stage 3. The patient is irreversibly comatose because the entire brain ceases functioning, but cardiovascular and pulmonary functions continue because they are maintained by artifical life support systems.

Stage 2. The patient is irreversibly comatose because the cerebral cortex has ceased functioning but the brainstem is still active, so that the cardiovascular and pulmonary functions continue.

Stage 1. The dying patient is conscious and in pain and desires to be in Stage 4.

Here Mayo and Wikler separate the biologic from the valuational or moral dimension. That persons in Stages 1 to 3 are alive is a biologic fact. But it is a value question whether we should keep them alive. Only Stage 4 constitutes death, properly understood, but our respect for the patient's autonomy should place the burden of proof on those who would paternalistically intervene in preventing the patient from going from Stage 1 to Stage 4. In Stage 2, the case of irreversible coma, we are absolved of any duty to preserve life since it has lost what is valuable about humanity. The same goes for Stage 3. The patient should be detached from the artificial maintenance and left to die.

So what should we do about the tragic blessing of biomedical technology with its ability to keep the organism, but not the mind, alive indefinitely? If Mayo and Wikler are right, we should give up our notion of the sanctity of biologic life, and recognize that some lives are not worth living, including life as an organism in a persistent vegetative state. Although the irreversibly comatose being is biologically alive, it is no longer a life possessing any quality. If we see that personhood involves being self-conscious, we may say in these cases that although the body is alive, the *person* is dead. Not only should the body be detached from expensive life-saving machines, but its organs should be removed for use on the living. Organs are a precious medical resource that can be used to enable people to live longer and better.

Indeed, you might conclude that this reasoning entails a presumption of organ removal in irreversibly comatose patients, to be overridden only by the expressed wishes of the person when he or she was alive. That is, given suitable public education, we should realize that the organs of the irretrievably comatose or dead should be used to help the living.

Just as the United States Supreme Court has ruled that a dying person can give advance notice that should he or she become irreversibly comatose, all life support systems should be removed, so likewise our living wills should have provisions in them directing that our organs be removed for transplantation while we are in such a state. In this case the immediate cause of death should be recorded as the donation of vital organs rather than removal of life support. This should be the next step in the attempt to make moral use of our technologic wonders. Eventually, a presumption in favor of transplanting organs from brain dead and neocortical dead patients would be recognized.

The response of the definitional reformers to all this is that the term *death* already has value connotations with the public, so that in including the permanent loss of consciousness in the definition of death, we are preserving what is practically valuable about the concept.

This response needs careful consideration. It may, in the end, be the right way to go. Nonetheless, clarity of thought inclines us to separate the biologic fact of death from the valuational and admit that a body with a dead cerebrum but a living brainstem is still biologically alive. Perhaps we need two locutions, "biologic death" and "person death," to preserve the integrity of meaning. So long as we see the issue clearly, the names don't matter.

Finally, let's look back on the problem cases mentioned at the beginning of this chapter. In the case of the New York woman who was beaten until she was irreversibly comatose, the assailant robbed her of all that was valuable to her as a person. This is just as evil as if he had killed her. We need a new concept for rendering a person permanently comatose, but the punishment should be equal to that given to a murderer.

Likewise, in *Grey v. Swayer* the law must recognize irreversible loss of consciousness as tantamount to death. If it had to decide between the two parties, it should have made the opposite award, for a body without a head cannot be conscious.

In Bruce Tucker's case, due process was violated. His family should have been notified, and the electroencephalogram reapplied several hours later. Even though the doctors were correct in wanting to transplant Tucker's heart and kidneys, the laws in place would have given his brother William the right to veto that desire. Doubtless the hospital was unwise in permitting the procedure.

Whether people like William Tucker, who believe that a breathing body is still a person, should be allowed to veto what society's experts decide to be rational procedure, is a difficult issue. Given our commitment to democratic processes, it is hard to see how we could justly override these vetoes, at least until a consensus is formed in society for such an override. That is one of the challenges of our time—to educate the public to the importance of quality concerns without destroying a basic commitment to the preservation of life. On one hand, we need to reject the absolutism of the Sanctity of Life Principle. On the other hand, we need to respect a basic presumption in favor of life as the basis of all other values. This is not an easy set of distinctions, but that's just why the process of coming to a clearer understanding is a challenge.

Study Questions

1. Discuss the four definitions of death. Which seems nearest to the truth? Why?

2. Discuss Mayo and Wikler's four stages of the human organism and their implications for our view of death. How cogent is their argument?

3. Since body organs are a scarce natural resource, should our policy be changed to allow the removal of the organs from the patient as soon as he or she dies (or while the dying person is unconscious or brain dead)? What are the arguments for and against this policy?

Endnotes

1. Cited in H. Tristram Engelhardt, Jr., *The Foundations of Bioethics* (Oxford: Oxford University Press, 1986), pp. 209f.

2. Cited in Robert M. Veatch, *Death, Dying, and the Biological Revolution* (New Haven: Yale, 1976), pp. 21–24.

3. Immanuel Jakobovitz, *Jewish Medical Ethics* (Philadelphia: Block, 1959), p. 277.

4. Quoted in Thomas Beauchamp and Seymour Perlin, eds., *Ethical Issues in Death and Dying* (Englewood Cliffs, N.J.: Prentice Hall, 1978), p. 14.

5. Roland Puccetti, "Brain Transplantation and Personal Identity," *Analysis* 29 (1969), p. 65. Engelhardt restates Puccetti's motto, "If the cerebrum is dead, the person is dead." (Engelhardt, op. cit., p. 211).

6. Engelhardt, op cit., p. 211.
7. Engelhardt, op cit., p. 53.
8. David J. Mayo and Daniel Wikler, "Euthanasia and the Transition from Life to Death," in Thomas Mappes and Jane Zembaty, eds., *Biomedical Ethics* (New York: McGraw Hill, 1986), pp. 400–408.

SELECTED BIBLIOGRAPHY

Code: D = Deontological; U = Utilitarian; C = Contractualist or Egoist; O = Objectivist; R = Relativist.

I. ETHICAL THEORY

Baier, Kurt. *The Moral Point of View.* Ithaca, N.Y.: Cornell University Press, 1958. This influential work sees morality primarily in terms of social control. (C) (O)

Dawkins, Richard. *The Selfish Gene.* 2nd ed. Oxford: Oxford University Press, 1989. One of the most fascinating studies on the subject, defending limited altruism from the perspective of self-interest (a type of C)

Frankena, William K. Ethics. 2nd ed. Englewood Cliffs, N.J.: Prentice-Hall, 1973. A succinct, reliable guide. (D) (O—Intuitionism)

Gert, Bernard. *Morality: A New Justification of the Moral Rules.* 2nd ed. Oxford: Oxford University Press, 1988. A clear and comprehensive discussion of the nature of morality. (C)

Hobbes, Thomas. *Leviathan* (1651). Indianapolis: Bobbs Merrill, 1958, Parts I and II. Classic work in Contractarian ethics.

Kant, Immanuel. *Foundations of the Metaphysics of Morals.* Lewis White Beck, trans. Indianapolis: Bobbs-Merrill, 1959. A classic work in D.

MacIntyre, Alasdair. *A Short History of Ethics.* London: Macmillan, 1966. A lucid, if uneven, survey of the history of Western ethics.

Mackie, J. L. *Ethics: Inventing Right and Wrong.* London: Penguin, 1976. A modern classic defense of relativism. (R)

Mill, John Stuart. *Utilitarianism.* Indianapolis: Bobbs-Merrill, 1957. A classic work in U.

Nielsen, Kai. *Ethics without God.* Buffalo: Prometheus, 1973. A very accessible defense of secular morality. (U)

Pojman, Louis. *Ethical Theory: Classical and Contemporary Readings.* Belmont, Calif.: Wadsworth,1989. An anthology containing readings on all the major positions.

———. *Ethics: Discovering Right and Wrong.* Belmont, Calif., Wadsworth, 1989. An objectivist perspective. (O)

Quinton, Anthony. *Utilitarian Ethics.* London: Macmillan, 1973. A clear exposition of classic Utilitarianism.

Rachels, James. *The Elements of Moral Philosophy.* New York: Random House, 1986. One of the clearest introductions to moral philosophy.

Singer, Peter. *The Expanding Circle: Ethics and Sociobiology.* Oxford: Oxford University Press, 1983. A fascinating attempt to relate ethics to sociobiology. (U)

Taylor, Richard. *Good and Evil.* Buffalo: Prometheus, 1970. A lively, easy to read work that sees the main role of morality to be the resolution of conflicts of interest. (C) (R)

Van Wyk, Robert. *Introduction to Ethics.* New York: St. Martin's Press, 1990. A clearly written recent introduction to the subject. (O) (attacks versions of C—minimal morality)

II. APPLIED ETHICS

Aiken, William and Hugh LaFollette. *World Hunger and Moral Responsibility.* Englewood Cliffs, N.J.: Prentice-Hall, 1977. The best collection of essays on the philosophical implications of world hunger.

Battin, Margaret Pabst and David Mayo, eds. *Suicide: The Philosophical Issues.* New York: St. Martin's Press, 1980. A set of contemporary essays, especially those by Brandt, Mayo, Martin, and Battin.

Beauchamp, Tom L. and Seymour Perlin, eds. *Ethical Issues in Death and Dying.* Englewood Cliffs, N.J.: Prentice-Hall, 1978. The best collection of essays on the subject.

Beauchamp, Tom L. and James F. Childress. *Principles of Biomedical Ethics.* 2nd ed. Oxford: Oxford University Press, 1983. An accessible work showing how ethical theory applies to issues in medical ethics.

Bedau, Hugo Adam, ed. *The Death Penalty in America.* 3rd ed. New York: Oxford, 1982. A helpful set of readings, reflecting all aspects of the contemporary debate.

Berns, Walter. *For Capital Punishment: The Inevitability of Caprice and Mistake.* New York: Norton, 1974. A retributivist defense of capital punishment.

Devine, Philip E. *The Ethics of Homicide.* Ithaca, N.Y.: Cornell University Press, 1978. The best treatment from a conservative perspective of the issues discussed in this book.

Feinberg, Joel, ed. *The Problem of Abortion.* Belmont, Calif.: Wadsworth, 1973. A valuable anthology, containing classic articles.

Frey, R. G. *Rights, Killing and Suffering.* Oxford: Basil Blackwell, 1983. The best work opposing animal rights.

Gerber, Rudolph and Patrick McAnany, eds. *Contemporary Punishment.* Notre Dame: University of Notre Dame Press. A helpful anthology with important articles by Hart, Wasserstrom, Flew, Mabbott, Packer, Menninger, Lewis, and others.

Glover, Jonathan. *Causing Death and Saving Lives.* London: Penguin, 1977. A U examination of several moral problems.

Hardin, Garrett. "Lifeboat Ethics: The Case Against Helping the Poor." *Psychology Today* (1974), reprinted in Aiken and LaFollette, op. cit. A modern classic of the Neo-Malthusian perspective.

Harris, John. *The Value of Life.* London: Routledge & Kegan Paul, 1985. A succinct but penetrating work in medical ethics, covering many of the topics discussed in this book.

Kleinig. *Valuing Life.* Princeton: Princeton University Press, 1991. The most thorough study of the value of life.

Kohl, Marvin, ed. *Beneficent Euthanasia*. Buffalo: Prometheus, 1975. An excellent collections of articles.

Lackey, Douglas. *The Ethics of War and Peace*. Englewood Cliffs, N.J.: Prentice Hall, 1989. A clear-headed discussion of pacifism and the just war theory.

———. *Moral Principles and Nuclear Weapons*. Totowa, N.J.: Rowman and Allenheld, 1984. A comprehensive study of the moral aspects of nuclear arms policy.

Ladd, John, ed. *Ethical Issues Relating to Life and Death*. Oxford: Oxford University Press, 1979. Contains nine important articles.

Mappes, Thomas and Jane Zembaty, eds. *Social Ethics*. 3rd ed. New York: McGraw Hill, 1986. An excellent anthology with succinct selections on most of the issues discussed in this book.

———, eds. *Biomedical Ethics*. 2nd ed. New York.: McGraw-Hill, 1986. An excellent set of readings on abortion, euthanasia, and the concept of death.

Menninger, Karl. *The Crime of Punishment*. New York: Viking Press, 1968. A defense of rehabilitation as a way of dealing with criminals.

Munson, Ronald, ed. *Intervention and Reflection*. Belmont, Calif.: Wadsworth, 1987. One of the best anthologies in medical ethics, especially on abortion and euthanasia.

Murphy, Jeffrie, ed. *Punishment and Rehabilitation*. 2nd ed. Belmont, Calif.: Wadsworth, 1985. An excellent collection of articles on the subject of punishment and its alternatives.

O'Neill, Onora. *Faces of Hunger*. Allen & Unwin, 1986. A careful Kantian discussion of the principles and problems surrounding world hunger.

Perlin, Seymour, ed. *A Handbook for the Study of Suicide*. Oxford: Oxford University Press, 1975. A helpful series of articles.

Pojman, Louis, ed. *Life and Death: An Anthology*. Boston: Jones & Bartlett, 1992. A companion to this book, containing readings on every topic discussed here.

Rachels, James. *Created From Animals: The Moral Implications of Darwinism*. Oxford: Oxford University Press, 1990. A provocative study with relevance to the issue of the sanctity of life and animal rights.

———. *The End of Life*. New York: Oxford University Press, 1986. A clear defense of voluntary active euthanasia.

Regan, Tom. *The Case for Animal Rights*. Berkeley: University of California, 1983. The most comprehensive philosophical treatise in favor of animal rights.

———, ed. *Matters of Life and Death*. New York: Random House, 1980. An excellent set of essays on euthanasia, suicide, war, capital punishment, animal rights, and environmental ethics.

Regan, Tom and Peter Singer, eds. *Animal Rights and Human Obligations*. Englewood Cliffs, N.J.: Prentice Hall, 1976. The best anthology on animal rights.

Robbins, John. *Diet for a New America: How Your Food Choices Affect Your Health, Happiness and the Future of Life on Earth*. Walpole, N.H.: Stillpoint, 1987. A strong case for vegetarianism.

Rohr, Janelle, ed. *Animal Rights: Opposing Viewpoints.* San Diego: Greenhaven Press, 1989. Elementary essays on the subject.

Schell, Jonathan. *Fate of the Earth.* New York: Knopf, 1982. An excellent book on the dangers of nuclear war.

Simon, Arthur. *Bread for the World.* Mahway, N.J.: Paulist Press, 1975. A poignant discussion of the problem of world hunger and some thoughtful suggestions for improving the situation.

Singer, Peter. *Practical Ethics.* Cambridge: Cambridge University Press, 1979. A helpful U approach.

———. *Animal Liberation.* 2nd ed. New York: New York Review of Books, 1990. The classic work on the subject. The second edition contains recent data on animal experimentation and factory farming.

Sorell, Tom. *Moral Theory and Capital Punishment.* Oxford: Blackwell, 1987. A clearly written, thoughtful work for the beginning student.

Sterba, James, ed. *The Ethics of War and Nuclear Deterrence.* Belmont, Calif.: Wadsworth, 1985. The best anthology on the subject.

Stoessinger, John G. *Why Nations Go to War.* 4th ed. New York: St. Martin's Press, 1985. A fascinating essay on the causes of war in the twentieth-century.

Szumski, Bonnie, Lynn Hall, and Susan Bursell, eds. *The Death Penalty: Opposing Viewpoints.* St. Paul: Greenhaven Press, 1986. Contains short but important articles. Basic.

Tooley, Michael. *Abortion and Infanticide.* Oxford: Oxford University Press, 1983. A sustained case for a liberal position on abortion.

VandeVeer, Donald and Christine Pierce, eds. *People, Penguins and Plastic Trees.* Belmont, Calif.: Wadsworth, 1990. A good set of readings on environmental issues, including animal rights.

Veatch, Robert M. *Death, Dying and the Biological Revolution.* New Haven: Yale University Press, 1976. A thoughtful discussion of issues relating to death and dying.

Walzer, Michael. *Just and Unjust Wars.* London: Penguin, 1977. A penetrating, and very readable study of morality and war.

Wasserstrom, Richard, ed. *War and Morality.* Belmont, Calif.: Wadsworth, 1970. Contains excellent articles.

Index